T0286812

Cambridge Elements ☰

Elements in Global Development Studies
edited by
Peter Ho
Zhejiang University
Servaas Storm
Delft University of Technology

GLOBAL HEALTH WORKER MIGRATION

Problems and Solutions

Margaret Walton-Roberts
Wilfrid Laurier University, Canada

CAMBRIDGE
UNIVERSITY PRESS

Shaftesbury Road, Cambridge CB2 8EA, United Kingdom

One Liberty Plaza, 20th Floor, New York, NY 10006, USA

477 Williamstown Road, Port Melbourne, VIC 3207, Australia

314–321, 3rd Floor, Plot 3, Splendor Forum, Jasola District Centre,
New Delhi – 110025, India

103 Penang Road, #05–06/07, Visioncrest Commercial, Singapore 238467

Cambridge University Press is part of Cambridge University Press & Assessment,
a department of the University of Cambridge.

We share the University's mission to contribute to society through the pursuit of
education, learning and research at the highest international levels of excellence.

www.cambridge.org
Information on this title: www.cambridge.org/9781009217798

DOI: 10.1017/9781009217781

© Margaret Walton- Roberts 2023

This publication is in copyright. Subject to statutory exception and to the provisions
of relevant collective licensing agreements, no reproduction of any part may take
place without the written permission of Cambridge University Press & Assessment.

First published 2023

A catalogue record for this publication is available from the British Library.

ISBN 978-1-009-21779-8 Paperback
ISSN 2634-0313 (online)
ISSN 2634-0305 (print)

Cambridge University Press & Assessment has no responsibility for the persistence
or accuracy of URLs for external or third-party internet websites referred to in this
publication and does not guarantee that any content on such websites is, or will
remain, accurate or appropriate.

Global Health Worker Migration

Problems and Solutions

Elements in Global Development Studies

DOI: 10.1017/9781009217781
First published online: June 2023

Margaret Walton-Roberts
Wilfrid Laurier University, Canada

Author for correspondence: Margaret Walton-Roberts, mwalton
roberts@wlu.ca

Abstract: International skilled health worker migration is a key feature of the global economy, a major contributor to socio-economic development and reflective of the transnationalization of health and elder care that is underway in most Organisation for Economic Co-operation and Development nations. The distribution of care and health workforce planning has previously been analyzed solely within national contexts, but increasingly scholars have shown how care deficits are being addressed through transnational responses. This Element examines the complex processes that feed health worker migrants into global circulation, the losses and gains associated with such mobility and examples of good practices, where migrants, sending and destination communities experience the best possible outcomes. It will approach this issue through the lens of problems, and solutions, making connections across the micro, meso and macro within and across the sections.

This Element also has a video abstract: www.cambridge.org/waltonroberts

Keywords: global health, health workers, care, feminist, migration

© Margaret Walton- Roberts 2023

ISBNs: 9781009217798 (PB), 9781009217781 (OC)
ISSNs: 2634-0313 (online), 2634-0305 (print)

Contents

1 Introduction: The Global Mobility of Healthcare Workers

1.1 Introduction

Health professionals are one of the key labour market sectors open to international transfer. The number of immigrant doctors and nurses working in Organisation for Economic Co-operation and Development (OECD) nations has increased 60 per cent between 2005 and 2015, from 1.1 million to 1.8 million (World Health Organization; WHO 2017a). Nursing in particular presents one occupational group where skilled labour exit is evident (Kingma 2006). Indeed, the opportunities for overseas migration are often one of the main reasons candidates enter the nursing profession in the first place (Walton-Roberts et al. 2017a). These workers generally seek a better life for themselves and their families, and in the process of their migration, they contribute to an ongoing differentiation of the healthcare delivery map by concentrating human health resources in core economies. Structural processes determine the variable conditions of work in different places (conditions of work, investments in health systems, the status and rights of health workers), and this frames health workers' migration decisions. This section introduces the issue of health worker migration. Beginning from a historical perspective, we see how the legacy of colonialism is evident in the geographies of migration pathways and the hierarchies embedded within healthcare occupations and systems. We consider new geographies and temporalities of health worker migration that reveal the increasingly complex processes that frame the global distribution and circulation of health workers today. We then consider how health worker migration became a global social policy issue of concern for multilateral institutions such as the International Labour Organization (ILO), the World Health Organization (WHO) and the United Nations (UN). Multilateral interventions have resulted in the landmark 2010 WHO Global Code of Practice on the international recruitment of health personnel.[1] This voluntary code aims to establish and promote principles and practices for the ethical international recruitment of health workers and to facilitate the strengthening of health systems (WHO 2010a). We explore these efforts at governing health worker migration. This section closes by considering some of the wider system issues health worker mobility raises, including how it relates to the promotion of universal health coverage (UHC) and how it is embedded in the sustainable development goals (SDGs), humanities' aspirational goals for a better world in 2030.[2]

---

[1] www.who.int/hrh/migration/code/WHO_global_code_of_practice_EN.pdf.
[2] https://sdgs.un.org/goals.

1.2 Origins, Growth and Significance of Global Health Worker Migration

Florence Nightingale is considered the mother of modern nursing. Her life and legacy are instructive for our interests since they represent two enduring features relevant to the global migration of nurses and other healthcare workers, the lasting influence of colonial geographies and hierarchies and the denial and misrepresentation of women's intellectual contributions to healthcare delivery and leadership. Nightingale's career reflects Britain's colonial and military history, and recognition of her prodigious contribution to nursing, and social policy more generally, remains eclipsed by sexist reviews of her work (cf Hogan 2020). As Lynn McDonald (2010), the editor of a sixteen-volume collection[3] of Nightingale's works has argued, Nightingale has earned the fame but not the respect that she deserves. The legacy of Nightingale aligns with the global mobility of nurses; both are features of the modern age. The colonial origins and extensive mobility of Nightingale's nursing career echo today in the reality that gaining a nursing credential is akin to acquiring a "passport" for emigration (Connell 2014). Such mobility and gender representation remain prominent in the contemporary era, in that over 80 per cent of nurses are women and the share of immigrants in the nursing workforce in OECD nations ranges from 5 per cent in France to 25 per cent in New Zealand.[4] Alongside increasing numbers of migrant health workers, the spatial and temporal patterns of health worker mobility have diversified. This mobility, in all its complexity, unsettles notions of *national* health systems, in no small part due to the international composition of the health workforce.

Nightingale's legacy continues to be intensely debated because of her support for British empire and colonialism, and her paternalist and racist views of Indigenous communities. In 2020 an article in *Nursing New Zealand* argued that continuing to venerate Nightingale was "disrespectful and painful" and that "Raising her as the beacon for nursing globally causes trauma and re-ignites the history and pain of colonialism" (Brookes & Nuku 2020, p. 35). Engaging a deeper understanding of colonialism is therefore central to contemporary analysis of this phenomenon. Critical engagement with what can be called the "colonial remnant" (Kwete et al. 2022), contextualizes not just health worker migration, but global health itself: "Decolonization as a process is still an unfinished agenda in today's world and global health is a mere reflection of this fact" (Kwete et al. 2022, p. 2). Kwete et al. (2022) suggest systematic

---

[3] www.wlupress.wlu.ca/Series/C/Collected-Works-of-Florence-Nightingale.
[4] https://migrationdataportal.org/themes/migration-data-relevant-covid-19-pandemic.

attempts to recognize these colonial remnants in global health need to occur at three levels, that of practices, the institutional/organizational and at the policy level. This section offers a review of some of these colonial remnants.

1.2.1 Geographies of Health Worker Migration

The development of healthcare systems was core to the "civilizing" mission of colonial expansion, as well as central to the success of military campaigns (Arnold 1993). War necessitated care for military personnel, and nursing personnel and medical science approaches spread with colonial military and missionary activities. British colonialism saw the spread of allopathic curative health and nursing traditions from the British Isles to colonial outposts such as India, resulting in outcomes marked by medical pluralism representing both colonial authority and Indigenous resistance (Bala 2012), to the benign neglect and reproduction of the poor status of nursing (Healey 2010). In the process, social hierarchies and understandings of healthcare traditions were transplanted into societies with their own specific cultural norms and histories of care. Nursing traditions fanned out from the core of colonial empire in the late 1800s and by the early 1900s, the United Kingdom (UK) and the United States of America (USA) had become active in promoting a certain vision of nursing professionalization that reflected hierarchies of race, nationality, gender and religion. The vision of nursing professionalization promoted in the UK quickly spread to the "colonies" of Canada, Australia, New Zealand, Ireland and then beyond.

The post-World War II (WW II) period saw the flow of nursing labour reverse away from arrival in the colonies to one that drew labour out of the colonies to be stratified into the health systems of high-income states. Starting with the formation of the National Health Service (NHS) in the UK, this public health system relied on the incorporation of medical and nursing professionals trained in South Asia, the Caribbean and African states. Trained through the "benevolence" of the civilizing mission, colonial systems reversed the movement of health workers during the post- WW II period to the enormous benefit of high-income nations. The launch of the NHS resulted in a massive expansion of demand for the inclusion of health workers from the edge of Empire into the British National Health System. This integration, however, remained marked by hierarchies, reflecting a stratified and segmented process organized by those in power in the core. For example, nurses trained in the colonies were positioned as lower ranked than British nurses, and this became concretized through training regulations and hierarchies that articulated with citizenship differences. Rafferty and Solano (2007) detail the creation of the Colonial Nursing Service, which directed British nurses to various parts of the Empire. They identify how in the post-1945 period the directional flow of this chain reversed as the needs of the UK's NHS exceeded the domestic supply of nurses. Controlled through the UK's 1943 Nurses' Act, the creation of the "nurse assistant" position placed foreign-trained nurses in subservient positions vis-à-vis British trained nurses. Colonialism, therefore, created and reinforced a relationship of inequality both at home and overseas for nurses trained in the colonies, but later drawn into the UK. Immigrant physicians who were trained in South Asia, Africa and the Caribbean and found employment in the NHS were often concentrated in the sectors least favoured by UK citizens. This included general practice, especially beyond the metropolis, and geriatrics, a speciality that did not formally exist in the UK until marginalized immigrant doctors developed it through their ground-breaking work (Raghuram et al. 2011). In Canada, the rise of Medicare in the 1960s depended upon the incorporation of foreign-trained health professionals, and by 1984 one-third of all doctors in Canada were immigrants (Mullally & Wright 2020).

In the 1960s, rapid economic development and expanding opportunities for women meant that the traditional work of nursing was increasingly less attractive. As health systems expanded, demand for nursing personnel exceeded domestic supply and drove countries such as the USA and Germany to seek workers from Asia. Education and training contributions from core nations, initially offered as philanthropy and development assistance, now emerged as a labour market primer that created a surplus to feed into the core nations to service their healthcare needs. The USA called upon neocolonial linkages to draw in nurses whose training they had helped to forge through Rockefeller Foundation investments. Catherine Choy (2003) has documented how the USA's active role in promoting nursing education in the Philippines eventually created a perpetual source of care labour that the USA drew upon for its own demands. During this time international agencies of the UN and ILO became attentive to the growing significance of international medical migration, and how it intersected with the fields of development, education and health (Yeates & Pillinger 2019).

By the 1970s the pattern was generally cast in terms of the migratory routes of healthcare workers. Ex-colonies became the source from which core nations drew in trained health workers. The post-colonial period saw some newly independent nations participate in the provisioning function of this global supply system. Doctors, nurses and other health professionals from these lower-income countries were attracted to higher-income nations, the apex of which include the USA, and the UK in Anglophone circuits, and France and Portugal within the Francophone and Lusophone circuits. Growing settler colonies such as Canada and Australia were also active participants, together with parts of Europe, including Germany, which recruited Korean nurses as guest workers, while portraying this as development assistance (Jung 2018). By the 1970s this process was increasingly cast as one of resource extraction from underdeveloped nations to high-income nations. Moreover, it was increasingly common for migrant health professionals to be stratified into lower positions in the occupational hierarchy in destination countries. Occupational and geographical stratification was, and remains, a common experience for immigrant healthcare professionals; working in poorer and less serviced communities (Reddy 2015), and in occupational sectors less attractive to domestically trained health workers (Raghuram et al. 2011).

In the Lusophone context, Angolan and Mozambican immigrants moved to Portugal in the late 1970s to escape civil conflict, and this included physicians who tended to be underutilized and employed below their skill level (Eaton 2003). Lusophone Africa (where the Portuguese language is spoken) includes Angola, Cape Verde, Guinea-Bissau, Mozambique, São Tomé, and Príncipe and, Equatorial Guinea. African regional migration agreements (including Portuguese-speaking nations) have increasingly focused on intra-regional mobility accords (including visa-free travel), but these have vacillated in response to economic decline and rising xenophobia (Adepoju 2001). Middle-class Brazilian immigrants to Portugal also benefitted from various twentieth-century reciprocal labour rights accords, yet by the 1990s conflict over the recognition of Brazilian dentists' credentials working in Portugal resulted in profound diplomatic tension over non-reciprocity. This was eventually resolved with a specific dispensation requiring supplementary training for Brazilian dentists, a case that marked a "rupture in the paradigm of reciprocal treatment" but was "consistent with colonial disjunctures ... " (Torresan 2021, p. 181). Francophone migration circuits include one between Quebec and France governed by The Quebec-France Agreement, which allows a person who has training and a permit to practice a regulated profession or trade in one partner territory, to have their skills recognized to be able to work in the other. Mutual recognition includes nurses, midwives, doctors, pharmacists and other allied health occupations.[5]

The 1970s also saw the emergence of Petro-states drawing in internationally trained health workers. After the Organisation of the Petroleum Exporting Countries increased oil prices, oil-producing states in the Middle East embarked on elaborate development agendas that included rapid expansion of their

---

[5] www.quebec.ca/emploi/reconnaissance-des-etudes-et-de-lexperience/faire-reconnaitre-son-experience/entente-quebec-france.

healthcare systems. Countries such as Saudi Arabia and United Arab Emirates (UAE) became new nodes in healthcare worker migration routes. Asian countries including India, Pakistan and the Philippines provided medical personnel to these expanding health systems, which relied on English as the working language, and thus these nodes became part of a wider Anglophone migration system (Percot 2006).

Considering this expanding circulation of health workers from lower- to higher-income nations, the brain drain argument became more intense into the 1990s, when Nelson Mandela berated the UK government for poaching South African nurses (Martineau et al. 2002).[6] As President of South Africa, he watched as the nation struggled with the AIDS epidemic and health workers fled to work in higher-income nations. The reality of lower-income nations using their resources to train health professionals, and then watching as they exited to plug the holes in high-income nations, was seen as unjust, immoral and a perverse subsidy (Mackintosh et al. 2006). However, the justification for global action on this matter was limited in the closing decades of the twentieth century, considering the prevailing neoliberal tendencies that shaped global relations from 1980s onwards. The power of markets and the hegemony of "free" trade to determine international relations had made the training and migration of healthcare workers just another form of goods and services embedded in the global economic system. In some cases, states engaged in excess training of health-care workers as a form of labour export. This tapped into the tendency for migrants to remit income to their families, thereby improving the balance of payments for low-income labour-sending nations. The epitome of this is the Philippines, as the nation sought to address its fiscal challenges from the1970s onwards through an explicit labour export policy, one where nurses formed a central group of deployed workers (Choy 2003; Rodriguez 2010). It was also understandable why so many health workers from lower-income nations embraced international migration, since relative conditions of work and pay are better in higher-income nations. For example, Indian healthcare workers can earn incomes anywhere between 20 and 90 per cent more than their home earnings, and more depending on their speciality and country of settlement (George & Rhodes 2017). However, this exchange can potentially hollow out public health systems resulting in the continued decline of employment conditions, which acts as a key migration driver in low-income economies. Structural adjustment programs (SAPs) imposed by multilateral institutions such as the World Bank also initiate this public disinvestment (Lewis 2006). Not only were high-income nations

---

[6] www.theguardian.com/society/2005/may/18/politics.publicservices.

extracting health resources in the form of trained workers but they were also contributing to perpetuating the conditions of exit driving this global migration system.

Patterns of health worker migration are evident in terms of the Global South to Global North flows. Traditional colonial relations frame some of these migration corridors, such as the movement of nurses from the Philippines to the USA, doctors from India, Pakistan and parts of Africa to the UK, nurses from the Caribbean to both the UK and USA, and dentists from Brazil to Portugal. Pacific Islanders are also plugged into networks with Australia and New Zealand. This traditional pattern of movement from the Global South to North has been in place for most of the latter part of the twentieth century, but more recently, the geography of healthcare worker migration is becoming more complex.

1.2.2 Changing Dynamics of Health Worker Mobility to the Middle East from Asia, and from Eastern and Central Europe to Western Europe

The rise of the Petro-states in the post-1970s period created new lines of health worker mobility, including Global South to Western Asia networks, some of which reflect long-established trading networks. Emerging and lower-income nations have also entered the global trade in healthcare services by, among other things, seeking international standards accreditation to provide specialized quality health care at competitive prices relative to more developed and well-established markets (MacReady 2007). A lack of domestically trained professionals in emerging Gulf States necessitated the massive importation of international workers to staff health systems as domestic systems of training were being developed (Ennis & Walton-Roberts 2018). In Asia and the Middle East, this investment and the development of health systems "is, in effect, globalizing health care" (Crone 2008, p. 117). Such development has drawn heavily on India as a source for nurses (George 2005), as well as other South Asian countries such as Nepal (Adhikari 2019). Increased south–south migration across Africa is also evident (Crush et al. 2015). Consider that over one-fifth of medical graduates newly licensed to practice in Nigeria are internationally trained (half from Asia and half from Africa). Currently, the top sources for immigrant doctors in South Africa include Nigeria, the UK, Cuba and the Democratic Republic of the Congo. Also, in Trinidad and Tobago half of the doctors are foreign born and foreign trained (coming from India, Jamaica and Nigeria) (WHO 2017a). Within Europe the ascension of new Eastern European member states has seen an increase in the east-to-west movement, for example, nurses from Poland working in the UK. Internal north-to-north migration is also evident, in part as a response to ethical recruitment demands, but also reflecting specific circuits of mobility, such as English language migration circuits including the UK, Ireland, Canada, New Zealand, Australia and the USA, and Francophone recruitment by Quebec in France and Belgium.[7]

Increasingly complex patterns of mobility are emerging not just in terms of geography, but also in terms of temporality and directionality. The range of intermediaries involved in the global mobility of health workers contributes to novel forms of temporary worker placements, for example as locums or highly specialized surgical teams contract hired to complete specific surgeries (Crush 2022). In the UK's NHS, the increase of agency work includes foreign-born workers, with 34 per cent of NHS agency staff being foreign-born compared to 17 per cent of non-agency staff (Hudson-Sharp et al. 2017). Of all South African doctors registered in Ireland, only 20 per cent report that they work *only* in Ireland, suggesting they work across multiple jurisdictions (WHO 2017a). We should also add to this complexity growing internationalized and privatized medical education. For example, Indian medical students train in China and Russia (Yang 2018), and Canadians and Americans train in the Caribbean (Morgan et al. 2017). Assessing the basic outlines of health worker mobility under these changing conditions disrupts the traditional assumptions of national state (public) funding of national health education systems and highlights the challenges emerging to the traditional Anglophone educational hierarchy. Such changes are connecting diverse regions of the world through increasingly globally orientated models of health training, skills development and professional mobility (Kingma 2006; Percot 2006; Walton-Roberts 2014, 2015c).

Health worker migration is propelled by the globalization and marketization of health care, which is itself a form of mobility in terms of ideas, ideologies and discourses (Levitt & Rajaram 2013). As corporate healthcare delivery systems expand geographically to lower-cost locations, we appear to be moving towards "flat medicine" for certain socio-economic classes who select their treatment options from a global landscape of health service integration (Crone 2008). Healthcare workers become one more factor that is sourced and "plugged in" to these emerging health service nodes. Health workers, whose international migration is spurred on by differences in opportunity between national systems, are now also increasingly distributed between public and private systems within national contexts. Internationally oriented health systems seek health professionals with international training, and the circulation of medical professionals between Global North and South health systems transmits both skills

---

[7] https://ici.radio-canada.ca/nouvelle/1771017/recrutement-infirmieres-preposes-etranger-sante-quebec.

(Hagander et al. 2013) and ideas about the role of markets in the health system (Levitt & Rajaram 2013).

1.2.3 Global Social Policy Governance on International Health Worker Recruitment and Migration

Throughout the 1960s UN agencies focused on the significance of training and education systems in the production of skilled workers vital for development, particularly health workers. While initially focused on supply at the national level, the issue of international "brain drain" became apparent when assessments of the supply of skilled heath workers had to address the reality of worker outflows due to international migration. By the 1960s, United Nations Educational, Scientific and Cultural Organisation (UNESCO) and the ILO were addressing the issue of "brain drain," and in 1966 UNESCO proposed a model of compensation between sending and receiving nations as one approach. This principle of compensation has remained, "influential, if contested, over the longer term" (Yeates & Pillinger 2019, p. 35). The growing international demands for healthcare workers resulted in lower-income states' health educational investments funding a global labour supply mechanism. By the early 1970s the term "brain drain" was commonly used to identify the extraction of highly trained professionals such as doctors and engineers. The inclusion of nursing into this debate through key reports by Mejia et al. (1979) feminized this social policy field and provided an important meeting ground for the ILO and WHO to monitor this practice (Yeates & Pillinger 2019, p. 62).

By the 1990s the acute global maldistribution of health workers was evident, together with the realization that more effective health system development was unattainable without addressing the right balance and distribution of health workers. For example, sub-Saharan Africa continued to export nurses overseas even as the region faced a shortfall of 60,000 nurses (Packer et al. 2009). As the 1990s progressed there was greater acknowledgment of, and demand for, policies that addressed the global imbalance of health workers. As global interest and acknowledgment of the gravity of this issue emerged, the WHO became actively involved in the creation of the second multilateral instrument focused specifically on health workers (after the ILO's 1977 nursing personnel convention), the WHO Global Code of Practice on the International Recruitment of Health Personnel (Yeates & Pillinger 2019).

Due to the uneven geographical distribution of health workers and the necessity of adequate numbers of health workers for sustainable health systems, signatories to the WHO Code agree to engage in ethical international recruitment of health personnel as part of strengthening health systems. Subsequently, global health diplomacy was effective in the creation of a series of voluntary codes of conduct to discourage health worker migrant recruitment from countries experiencing crisis-level shortfalls in medical staffing (see Section 4 for more on codes). The WHO Global Code of Practice on the International Recruitment of Health Professionals (adopted in May 2010) is considered a landmark agreement that "suggests evolution in the capacity of the WHO Secretariat, Member States, and civil society to engage in global health 'law-making'" (Taylor & Dhillon 2011, p. 22).

One of the main motivations for voluntary codes is a desire for transnational social justice because the "brain drain" of health workers represents an inequitable distribution of training investments between sending and receiving regions. However, even in this area, the justice dimension of ethical codes is limited by the fact that in some cases out-migration is promoted by the sending state as a form of labour export policy (Rodriguez 2010). It is also difficult to characterize international migration as a problem when fiscally constrained health systems generate unemployed and underemployed health professionals in the source country (Lorenzo et al. 2007). Migration is also driven by families, and migrant social networks, and is often supported by the state for purposes of remittance generation, leading to the creation of a "migration culture" (Connell 2014). In such contexts, it may be difficult and impractical to curtail migration using voluntary codes.

Other types of mutual agreements accompany the globalization of health care, which is recursively spurred on by trade in health-related services under the World Trade Organization's General Agreement on Trade in Services (Smith et al. 2009). Regional economic and educational convergence processes (including bilateral agreements and Memoranda of Understanding (MOUs)) offer various approaches to expanding credential recognition regimes and promoting health worker mobility. We discuss regional bilateral agreements in more detail in Section 4.

1.3 System Issues

1.3.1 How Global Health Worker Migration Relates to the Goals of Universal Health Coverage

Universal Health Coverage (UHC) aims to create a system of coverage so that, "all people have access to the health services they need, when and where they need them, without financial hardship."[8] UHC is a major undertaking considering the inverse care law, in that the availability of healthcare services varies

---

[8] www.who.int/health-topics/universal-health-coverage#tab=tab_1.

inversely with the need for it, and this is more evident in cases where market forces are in operation (Hart 1971). Differential access to health service is very clear in rural versus urban centres, and increasingly we see the range, quality and availability of health services increase as we move up the urban hierarchy. In countries with poorly developed public health systems, income is especially determinate of the level of healthcare services accessible. There are also regional health hubs utilized by those seeking specialized care that provide patients who can afford it with more healthcare options. Overall a world marked by highly uneven economies produces uneven healthcare systems, and as health worker migration continues these inequities are worsened.

The world will not reach UHC without a sustained and significant investment in the health workforce, worker training, education and retention everywhere. Innovation, engagement with new technologies and new work and care models can enhance care practices and address workforce shortages and maldistribution and create more appropriate skill mixes that can help move countries towards UHC (Britnell 2019). Britnell argues that we need to reframe the health workforce debate as one of productivity and wealth creation, not cost. This has also been echoed by calls to invest in the care economy following the coronavirus disease 2019 (COVID-19) pandemic in the form of the Protect, Invest, Together campaign to #Supportheathcareworkers launched by the WHO in 2021.[9]

1.3.2 The Sustainable Development Goals

The SDGs relate to the global migration of health workers in multiple ways. Access to training (SDGs 4.3), orderly and responsible migration (10.7) and retention of health workers (3.c) are relevant to understanding the processes that drive international health worker migration, the experiences of those who engage in international migration and how this migration can be responsibly managed (Thompson & Walton-Roberts 2019). SDG 10 is aimed at reducing inequality within and among countries, which is a macro factor shaping the dynamics of global health worker migration in the form of Global South to the Global North movement. The negative impact of health worker emigration from low-income nations is evident in the transfer of resources invested in training, and the multiple losses incurred when experienced health professionals exit national health systems. This loss is compounded when internationally educated health workers struggle to find appropriate employment in the receiving country. SDGs target 10.7 calls to facilitate orderly, safe and responsible migration

---

[9] www.who.int/news/item/30-07-2021-health-workforce-in-covid-19-action-series-time-to-protect .-invest.-together.

and mobility of people, including through the implementation of planned and well-managed migration policies. Effective healthcare delivery depends on having the right number and mix of health workers in place. The international migration of healthcare workers needs to be monitored, since health workforce shortages can undermine equity across health systems. SDG 10.7 and the WHO's code on health worker recruitment offer some solutions that sending and receiving countries can follow to improve the experiences of health worker migrants, monitor and regulate the scale and scope of health worker migration, and enhance health systems in sending and receiving nations. The COVID-19 pandemic has both set back and reignited these challenges.

1.4 Conclusion

Immigration policy in many OECD nations now places a premium on migrants with specific skills that are seen as vital to national development (Gabriel 2013). This is particularly evident in healthcare systems, which have long relied on internationally educated medical staff to meet structural shortages (WHO 2010a). As health care has become increasingly globalized, health workers, including nurses, move substantial distances to provide care for patients (Clark et al. 2006; Walton-Roberts 2015c). The gender implications of this issue are particularly significant, since women account for an increasing proportion of all migrants, reaching almost half of today's 191 million international migrants. Female migrants are overrepresented in health and personal care sectors of the global economy, which are often undervalued in terms of income security and status (Valiani 2011). While the specific policy context of internationally educated nurses' (IENs) integration into different national labour markets varies (Picot & Sweetman 2011), there is a structural trajectory of convergence of feminized migrant health and care workers being incorporated into national health systems facing restructured or diminished state spending (Yeates 2009). Demographic and healthcare delivery change is also creating global markets for nursing and other health workers (Kingma 2006; Walton-Roberts 2015b; Connell & Walton-Roberts 2016). Linked to this global migration the related pressures exacted on professional standards and qualifications are important dimensions of the globalization of health, care and education and the restructuring of labour process hierarchies (Segouin et al. 2005; Baumann & Blyth 2008; Walton-Roberts 2015a).

International health worker mobility requires attention to complicated domestic and international politics, regulatory approaches, and governance. The health sector is particularly challenging because it touches on so many fundamental issues, from the quality of care to the way we have chosen to organize our respective healthcare systems. The degree of health professional regulatory organization, the relative power of professional domestic groups, and the degree of public support for these professions and the health system frame the level of interest and commitment to effectively integrate internationally trained healthcare workers. Health worker migration has been subjected to perhaps some of the most organized mechanisms of migration management through codes of ethical recruitment, skills exchanges and service exchange provisions. The costs of migration, the inability of individual countries to develop effective policies for worker retention and return, the role of recruiting (in what amounts to the institutionalization of migration) and the particular significance of health care – literally involving matters of life and death – has posed ethical challenges and resulted in international codes of practice controlling recruitment. As regional trade groups, such as the Association of Southeast Asian Nations (ASEAN), and "trade in natural persons" under the General Agreement on Trade in Services (GATS) Mode 4, increase in significance, new forms of mutuality and group dynamics will structure the international migration of health workers. The migration of health professionals is one of the nascent areas where we witness global governance migration frameworks emerging. COVID-19 has shown how important having the right number and mix of health workers is to secure global population health. This demands international cooperation, which can be achieved through global collaboration to meet UHC and the SDGs, but there are other examples of how nations address this problem. Migrant health workers are incorporated into an evolving geographically extended labour processes activated through global migration pathways and circuits. We will explore these issues in more detail in subsequent sections.

2 Feminist Political Economy and Global Care Chain Perspectives on Health Worker Migration

2.1 Introduction: Care as a Human Trait

The year 2020 was the one everyone became conscious of the importance and relevance of care in their and their loved ones' lives. The COVID-19 pandemic reminded us that as a relational species we depend upon the care of others at various stages of our lives, and a pandemic revealed where and when care mattered for many of us. In accessing basic resources, medical treatment, and interaction and support for daily living, the consequences of the pandemic (disease, isolation, social distancing) reaffirmed the centrality of care to our species' survival. For scholars and practitioners of care this was nothing new, but it did reassert how important care is for human well-being, and how far it has been undervalued in systems of market exchange. Despite the renewed talk of care, scholars argue that when it comes to state action and budget priorities, "carelessness continues to reign" as market logic and austerity take their toll on care infrastructures (Chatzidakis et al. 2020, p. 3). Indeed Chatzidakis et al. (2020, p. 7) in their *care manifesto* argue that many of the phenomena the world faces today, from climate change to Black Lives Matter, to the plight of refugees, are connected to "the market-driven lack of care at every level of society". In this section we review different theories of care that explore what care means and how it is delivered in different societies. We then consider what has been called the transnationalization of care, where care work in many high-income nations has been outsourced to women from lower-income nations through circuits of global care labour migration. Next, we consider more broadly the ethics of care. Finally, we then consider how care has become recentred to some degree, considering the coronavirus pandemic and explore some of the actions that have been announced by state governments and international organizations that offer a deeper appreciation of the centrality of care to our ability to collectively recover and "build back better."

2.2 Theories of Care

There are several models conceptualizing relations of care, including global chain chains, care diamonds and care pentagons (see Figure 1). Not surprisingly these models are based upon forms of relationality, in that care is about interaction and dependence between people, but they also communicate

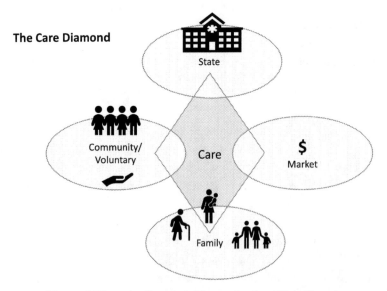

Figure 1 The care diamond (illustration by Alicia Pouw)

different types of spatial arrangement in terms of the scale, proximity and geography of care provision.

Care has long been understood as a devalued form of labour, primarily because of its association with women's work, and the idea that the provision of care is linked to women's natural or essential ability to care for others. As an essential trait, care has traditionally not been seen as a competency requiring any kind of skill or training. Care is also traditionally relegated to an extension of the domestic sphere, or social reproduction, and its contribution to the formal economic sphere has not been fully acknowledged or compensated. The care work women do globally for no or little pay contributes $10.8 trillion to the global economy (Coffey et al. 2020). This is equal to about half of the USA's entire gross domestic product in 2021. Under neoliberal market-based systems of organization this traditional devaluation of care continues and remains unvalued, under-resourced and un or poorly paid. De Silva (2017) suggests that the self will be the first preference in terms of who provides care (self-care), but this varies based on multiple factors. The care pentagon highlights the role of agency on the part of the care receiver, the changing context of local and transnational care giving within migrant families, and the way care receivers negotiate care with different agents based on notions of relationality.

How states have provided different forms of care has also included a growing outsourcing of care using migrant workers. There is evidence of older people being moved offshore to gain care in places where care labour is cheaper (Schwiter et al. 2020), but the more common and earlier practice of outsourcing care is through high-income nations' use of racialized or other marginalized immigrant women by drawing them into care networks through migration programs. For example, prior to WW II, some European domestic workers entered Canada as landed immigrants with a commitment to provide live-in care service for a set period of time (Bakan & Stasiulis 1997). Each new version of the migrant care giver scheme introduced in Canada imposed stricter residency rights and more limitations. These schemes reflect immense power imbalances between the sending and receiving states, and this kind of immigration policy effectively reproduces the exploitation and invisibilization of such care workers (Macklin 1991).

2.3 Transnationalized Care

The trajectories highlighted in Section 1 reveal how health and other forms of care (especially child and elder care) have become transnationalized as migrants, mostly women, and have been incorporated into wealthier states to provide care in sectors that are variously subject to austerity and underinvestment. By the late 1990s the increasing use of immigrant women as care givers in high-income nations was

The Global Care Chain

Figure 2 The global care chain (illustration by Alicia Pouw)

interpreted by feminist scholars as a new form of the international division of reproductive labour between middle-class women in high-income receiving countries, migrant domestic workers and poorer women unable to migrate from lower-income nations (Parreñas 2000). This connection was later interpreted as a form of Global Care Chain, a series of links between people across the globe based on paid or unpaid care work (Hochschild 2000) (see Figure 2). Women at the top end of the chain use migrant care workers to support them to work outside the home or for other reasons. The migrant women providing these services often leave their own family behind, and then pay other local women to look after their care demands, and so the chain goes on. This form of outsourcing of care became further understood as the transnationalized of care (Yeates 2011), that allowed high-income nations to underinvest in their own welfare state and use the undervalued labour of immigrant women to provide the care services their populations require (Ormond & Toyota 2018). These chains allow for the extraction of care based on the exploitation of multiple divisions including gender, ethnicity, class, nation and uneven development. The World Health Organization (WHO 2017b, p. 1) has referred to migrant women care workers as "a cushion for states that lack adequate public provision for long-term care, childcare and care for the sick", and identified a "care paradox," wherein migrant women work to fulfill the growing need for care workers in high-income and middle-income nations and strengthen weak health systems in these locations, while lacking health services themselves.

Further nuancing our understanding of how scale and spatial difference inform care, Parvati Raghuram (2012) examines care in diverse geographical contexts, and how place informs the context of care. Raghuram (2012) argues that research on care chains has not fully considered how the care diamonds that exist in migrant-sending regions will precondition people's expectations of what care giving and receiving should be after they have migrated, and how and by whom care might be provided. Raghuram (2012) uses India as an example to show how the state attempted to include marginalized groups into the developmentalist state not from a perspective of care, but from that of the modernization of the state. Likewise, the role of the church in colonialism and missionary work changed the conditions of work for caregivers but did not challenge notions of female subordination that are embedded in domestic work. This tension between worker's rights and care as religious benevolence continues to frame how migrant worker rights are advanced at the global scale within care diamonds. Place-based differences also inform how different groups of people are incorporated as carers within the care diamond, with different hierarchies and expectations attached to diverse groups of health and care workers in different geographical contexts. Raghuram (2012) illustrates how assumptions about the care diamond miss variables such as the variety of the family form, the presence of other transnational care actors, including various levels of state that provide different forms of insurance, and state regulation of nongovernmental organizations who provide care to marginalized populations. Integrating the care diamond and care chain approach also demands that we focus on patriarchy and the household in the Global North as well as the Global South and avoid the obsession of focusing only on the migrant women who move, rather than the institutions that are the beneficiaries of their labour.

Ortiga et al. (2021, p. 435) take up Raghuram's call to articulate care diamonds and chains, but they ask; "how does the care chain supply of migrant care workers reshape the contours of the local caregiving market and the experiences of local caregivers?" Using the case of Singapore, where the state engages in different "filtering" schemes to integrate migrant and domestic workers into elder care, Ortiga et al. (2021, p. 436) reveal "how skills regimes serve as an important meeting point in understanding how the global migration of care workers intersects with local issues of care." In effect, the migration and the care regime are brought together through the intersection of care diamonds (how care is organized between different actors within the national policy space), and care chains (migrant care worker mobility pathways and their state-regulated status and role in receiving countries) (see Figure 3). Local care contexts (including the public's expectations, state regulation and the nature of care delivery) frame the kind of skills and competencies care workers are understood to need, and the supply of care workers who can fill this demand is then informed by local labour supply and the migration regime or care chain that states' support or permit. In the case of Singapore, the family has been the main provider of elder care, and as care demands have increased families have turned to foreign domestic workers to help provide care. An aging Singaporean society has increased the pressure on care givers, leading the state to encourage citizens (mainly wives, mothers and retirees) to supplement community-based care, while also increasing the training expectations demanded of migrant workers (which has led to private organizations creating training programs both in

Figure 3 Global care chains intersecting care diamonds
(illustration by Alicia Pouw)

Singapore and in the sending country). Figure 3 presents an illustration of the interaction of the care chain and the care diamond.

2.4 Ethics of Care

Health care and care more broadly demand greater policy attention and consideration from an ethics of care perspective. Such a perspective recognizes the variable needs of human populations and the persistent truth that at different stages of life we all need to be cared for. Recognizing this, in 2002 the WHO sponsored a panel to consider "ethical choices in long term care: what does Justice require?" The summary of the WHO report acknowledged the role of family caregivers and noted that the limits of how care is being organized were being reached. The report encouraged states to consider "alternatives that do not depend on care based exclusively on either affection or market principles" (WHO 2002, p. 10). The suggested way forward was to include care as a primary good – a basic need that all humans require at some stage of their life – and change the idea of primary goods to that of capabilities, as this allows for a more accurate comparison of quality of life. This argument echoes Martha Albertson Fineman's (2008) work on vulnerability and the human condition, in that vulnerability is recognized as a universal constant of the human condition and necessitates models of state responsibility and responsiveness to this reality.

An interesting dimension of this WHO report on the ethics of care reveals an early recognition of what Yeates (2011) later termed the transnationalization of care:

> Much of the caregiving in wealthy and developed countries is being provided by care workers, nursing professionals, and others who have migrated from impoverished and developing countries. While these workers may experience economic benefit, they also create gaps in their own families and communities. Arguably, wealthy nations incur a debt in this exchange that somehow needs to be repaid. Likewise, it is reasonable to ask if the multinational

corporations that depend on the natural and human resources in developing countries have a responsibility to fill the gaps in caregiving they help to create. (WHO 2002, p. x).

The WHO report indicated the reality of this global provisioning of care, the problems sending nations face in servicing it and the responsibilities that should be incurred on the part of receiving nations who benefit from the global circulation of care labour. We can revisit that document considering the influence of the COVID-19 pandemic and consider the argument that: "Any societal commitment of resources to build institutions needs to be accompanied by a commitment to the basic human dignity of those who will use them." (WHO 2002, p. ix). This posits that the role of migrant care givers, particularly those employed on temporary visas, whose rights are limited, is central to understanding the ethics of how care is organized. Ethics of care debates, particularly in the context of the increasingly transnational organization of care delivery across many higher-income nations, are central to considerations of how we recover from the COVID-19 pandemic.

2.5 Building and Investing in Care Infrastructure: Pandemic Responses

Building and investing in care infrastructure has emerged as a significant policy goal in light of the COVID-19 pandemic. Building awareness of how health and care workers are globally sourced and circulated, and understanding the multiple consequences of this mobility, are key to this goal of investing in better care infrastructure. Debates on the ethic of care posit that care is a basic human need, that states should play a central role in the provision of such care, but that systems undervaluing care and those who provide it through the reproduction of various forms of inequity are both unsustainable and unethical. The pandemic has offered a moment of opportunity to reframe how societies value care. Such renewed attention and focus can be seen in various initiatives proposed by states and international organizations, a selection of which are provided below as examples of how the discourse on care is being reframed.

National governments have responded to the pandemic by proposing various spending initiatives on care issues, especially the undue burden women have faced because of the pandemic. The federal government of Canada has responded to the pandemic by supporting women and gender equality with $100 million Feminist Response and Recovery Fund. The government affirms the systemic and longstanding inequalities women and girls have experienced and recognizes that Canada needs critical recovery efforts to represent, support, and include women in leadership, workplace participation and economic security concerns. The representation of Indigenous women, Black women, women of colour and LGBTQ2 individuals is especially advocated through this response (Government of Canada 2021). The USA "Build Back Better Framework" has been launched to rebuild America's economy and workforce amidst the COVID-19 pandemic. The framework intends to grow the economy by enabling more Americans to "join and remain in the labor force." This initiative includes investment in childcare, care for older and disabled Americans, and support for the workers who contribute to these individuals' care. Additionally, the framework seeks to address climate change and expand affordable health care by reducing prescription costs, strengthening the afford- able care act and expanding on Medicaid coverage and Medicare benefits (White House 2021). The UK has released their plans for growth in response to the COVID-19 crisis which include plans for jobs, institutions, infrastructure, skill building, education, technology, financing and climate initiatives. This includes building and investing in care infrastructure through high-profile projects to develop new hospital programs and investing in giving people access to the skills, education and training needed to improve employment prospects and opportunities in health and social care (HM Treasury 2021). The UK's NHS has also released the NHS Long Term Plan in 2019 as a "10-year strategy for improving and reforming the NHS in England." The plan was set to improve the quality of care, expand primary and community services and reduce health inequalities. Considering the COVID-19 crisis, new demands have emerged for people's health and well-being along with the needs for building and investing in care infrastructure. The report lays out the progress the NHS hopes to achieve for care systems affected by the pandemic and how they have attempted to reduce inequalities during the COVID-19 crisis (Thorlby et al. 2021).

At the level of multilateral partnerships, USA President Biden has also been promoting a broader G7 leaders Build Back Better World Partnership to pro- mote infrastructure development in low- and middle-income countries. The Build Back Better World Partnership (B3 W) is global in scope and aims to narrow the discrepancies in climate, health and health security, digital technol- ogy, and gender equity and equality in low-income countries that have been exacerbated by the COVID-19 pandemic. The B3 W has been interpreted as a possible counter to China's massive belt and road investment approach (Meeks 2021).

The WHO and European Investment Bank (EIB) have sought to enhance their cooperation to support countries addressing the impact of COVID-19 on health care, healthcare workers, infrastructure, water, sanitation, hygiene and training availability and preparedness in vulnerable countries. These measures are aimed at reducing the health and social impact of future health emergencies.

Low- and middle-income countries will benefit from the financing and securing of medical supplies, health coverage and health infrastructure. The cooperation between the WHO and EIB in the first phase aims to provide funding to ten African countries as part of a global response to COVID-19 outside of the European Union (EU) (WHO 2020a).

The Economic and Social Commission for Asia and the Pacific (United Nations Economic and Social Commission for Asia and the Pacific 2021) has focused on the unpaid care economy through SDG 5, gender equality and the empowerment of all women and girls. The COVID-19 pandemic has intensified the risks and vulnerabilities for women and girls across the Asia-Pacific region. The work they have taken up, both as front-line healthcare workers and in their homes points to a need for policies to reduce and redistribute unpaid care work. Policies needed include building and investing in care infrastructure, care-related social protection transfers and benefits, care services and employment-related care policies.

The COVID-19 pandemic has impacted economies and societies of WHO member states significantly, but the South-East Asian (SEA) region has profoundly been affected due to longstanding gaps in health systems and essential health services. Thus, adequate investments through a sustained focus on achieving health-related SDGs and UHC is part of a strategy to build back better after COVID-19. Strengthening care infrastructure will reduce inequities experienced in the SEA region and allow care-oriented systems to better respond to emergencies (WHO 2021a).

The Asia-Pacific region has come together to examine the risks for vulnerable groups within countries and vulnerable countries with insufficient resources, capacity and infrastructures who should not be "left behind" during the COVID-19 crisis. To achieve the SDGs, especially in areas of poverty, decent work, education, health for women, migrant workers and other labourers, development gaps must be closed between countries. Policies in Asia and the Pacific are critical to ensuring care infrastructures in areas of digitalization and regional cooperation are developed. Therefore, pre-existing vulnerabilities magnified by the pandemic can begin to be addressed (Asia-Pacific SDG Partnership 2021).

The International Labour Organization (ILO 2021) affirms the increased gender inequality which has occurred because of the COVID-19 crisis and calls for new policies and measures to be taken by governments to make women's rights to work and labour a central focus of COVID-19 recovery plans. Gender gaps in care work are especially prominent, and globally women have seen a surge in ongoing workplace issues since the pandemic began. The ILO advocates that there is a lack of care services and infrastructure that supports women. In both the workforce and in unpaid care work in the household, women are disproportionately facing the brunt of the COVID-19 crisis. Investing in health, social work and education sectors can build on pre-existing care infrastructures and promote equality in the workforce.

The WHO, the International Council of Nurses (ICN) and The World Health Assembly (WHA) as a decision-making body of the WHO met with delegations from all 194 Member States and Non-State Actors to discuss "Ending this pandemic, preventing the next: building together a healthier, safer and fairer world." The resultant report focuses on the specifics of the WHA assembly meeting affecting nursing policy and global care agendas. In 2021, the WHA resolved to protect, safeguard, and invest in the health and care workforce, and to invest in care infrastructure protections. The COVID-19 crisis revealed that post-pandemic, more intense building and investment are needed in care systems and infrastructure to achieve the 2030 Agenda for Sustainable Development (ICN 2021).

Overall, these examples of plans to address the consequences of the COVID-19 pandemic and boost the effort to "build back better" recognize and prioritize the importance of care infrastructure, and within that also acknowledge the necessity of addressing the deeply gendered imbalances that exist in care work (paid and unpaid). The focus on care wrought by the consequence of a pandemic provides an important opportunity for national governments and international organizations to collaborate in the mobilization of resources to promote human well-being through health and care investments. These opportunities are also reflected in the convergence of global health and social development agendas such as the SDGs and the work of the WHO. The next section considers this in relation to the global migration and mobility of healthcare workers more specifically.

2.6 Conclusion

Care is a feature of human interaction that is central to our well-being as a species. At some point in the life cycle, we all need care and/or will be expected to provide it. Doing so, and the quality of the care we provide, is central to our ability to secure our well-being. Theories of care reveal phases of care provision and the different roles played by those who provide, receive and are responsible for care. Different actors are involved in care, as demonstrated in the care diamond. States create various contexts for care provision, and this plurality is organized in terms of the distribution of care between the state, the family, the market and community actors. The care pentagon includes the self as an important actor in the provision of care, and this role also varies spatially and temporally. Recent changes in how care is delivered through the care diamond or welfare state have seen higher-income nations outsource or transnationalize care provision using international migration. Global care chains now service care needs, and in the process, we witness global exploitation of uneven development and other markers of difference to fill care gaps that wealthier states have permitted to emerge. Connecting the nature of the care diamond with that of care chains allows us to see how states facilitate the incorporation of immigrant women into their particular care markets. These practices raise important concerns regarding the ethics of care, and the responsibilities of higher-income states to acknowledge the benefits they accrue from their exploitation of global uneven development through the incorporation of racialized immigrant women into their health and care sectors. In the next section we explore this process with reference to the problems associated with the global migration of healthcare workers

3 Health Worker Global Migration: Patterns, Processes and Problems

3.1 Introduction

Contemporary health worker migration patterns and processes are increasingly complex. The second round of reporting on the WHO Global Code of Practice on the International Recruitment of Health Personnel detailed the increased number of migrant doctors and nurses now working in OECD nations, the growing prominence of bilateral agreements between states facilitating and managing the mobility of health workers, and the increased diversity of migration routes and visa categories (temporary, circular, permanent, multistep) being used (WHO 2017a). The report argues that the WHO Code and member states' improved reporting on health worker migration our understanding and management of this mobility. The report offers five key lessons: (1) To varying degrees all countries are source and destination sites (e.g., Canada integrates migrant health workers and sees its own workers leave for other countries, especially the USA). (2) Effective policies on the integration of internationally trained health workers can be shared internationally. (3) Strategic linkages can and must be made across the health labour market: This includes production (training and education), licensing and registration (professional associations), employment and migration (state policies and practices). (4) That improved reporting and sharing of migration data through the WHO Global Code will provide a more complete global picture of health worker mobility. (5) That low- and middle-income countries receive targeted support to implement the Code. This relatively high-level view of the global migration of healthcare workers provides an indication of how important this form of human mobility is for global health development.

In this section we review the importance of healthcare workers to health systems, including how health workforce management approaches integrate internationally trained migrant healthcare workers. We then consider general approaches used to understand the migration and mobility of healthcare workers in terms of the drivers of migration, push, pull and network factors (including intermediaries and bilateral agreements), and labour market integration. We then examine the context for migration in terms of sending, receiving and transit contexts, while appreciating that places can function as all three of these simultaneously depending upon the migratory processes underway. We then review an important area of mobility that is relevant to understanding forms of health worker international mobility, that of health care workers who are "foreign trained" but not necessarily immigrants or "foreign born." This type of mobility reflects an increasing transnationalization of health professional training, with implications for how states might manage to meet the SDGs and UHC goals.

3.2 Healthcare Workers Are the Backbone of Health Systems

Healthcare workers are the backbone of any health system. The COVID-19 pandemic has revealed that health systems are not resilient, and this is in no small part due to workforce issues. Therefore, by addressing health workforce issues we are also addressing future health system resilience. Across the world, countries entered the COVID-19 pandemic with vastly different health workforce capacities, and the density of health workers to population (a key variable for revealing spatial inequalities in health systems over space and time) differed across and within countries. Campbell (2018) explores health worker density, migration and mobility globally, revealing that the African continent has the lowest density of all WHO regions. The report also demonstrates the complex patterns of mobility globally, with health worker migrants moving South to South, South to North as well as Intra-regionally. Regardless of these differences the pandemic has exhausted healthcare workers globally, and in several nations attrition rates are increasing as health professionals retire early and leave the profession. WHO Regional Office for Africa (2021b) guidance on how to manage workforce attrition suggests several recommendations for strengthening health systems in response to COVID-19. These include repurposing and mobilizing the existing workforce, changing working patterns, recalling inactive or retired health professionals back to the workforce, and calling on volunteers and workers from other sectors (military, private sector), including internationally trained healthcare workers who are not able to work for various reasons, including lack of licensing.

The numbers of international migrants are on the rise and in selected OECD countries the share of foreign-trained doctors and nurses increases. Moreover, the COVID-19 pandemic has resulted in many OECD countries taking steps to enable migrant healthcare workers to enter their health workforce system more quickly. The contributions of migrant doctors and nurses in OECD countries during the COVID-19 crisis have been documented by the OECD (2020) and are likely to increase as a consequence of the pandemic. A recent study of EU member states suggests healthcare systems are not resilient to shocks. Health systems across the world are now dealing with immense surgical and treatment backlogs that will depend upon a burnt-out workforce and thus will take years to clear. The inability to deal with staff and supply shortages before the pandemic was already evident across EU health systems and dealing with surge capacity on top of pre-existing strains in early phases of the pandemic added extra burdens. Violence against healthcare workers from antivaxxers and those opposed to public health measures have also exacted costs, including the need for police protection for some workers.

There is evidence of obvious under resourcing across EU health systems. In response what is needed is more healthcare worker investment, especially to avoid shortages in primary care, increase retention rates and enhance patient safety by improving working conditions (European Commission 2021). More broadly, researchers have argued that health systems must move from "just in time" health systems/workforce to "just in case" approaches to be prepared for the inevitable next pandemic, and to secure necessary supplies through the stockpiling of medical and PPE equipment (Barocas et al. 2021).

Health systems cannot serve patients well unless the workforce is looked after. What is needed is more sophisticated healthcare workforce planning, improved forecasting and planning capacities. Globally we need sustainable health workforces and deeper collaboration between states to develop better approaches to achieving this. High-income countries must be more responsible in terms of training health personnel domestically to achieve self-sufficiency, but if they do recruit health workers internationally, it must be done more ethically. The effective and equitable integration of internationally educated health professionals into the health systems of the countries they have migrated to is also profoundly consequential for health systems, patients and health workers in countries of origin, destination and transit. To understand the global migration of health workers in more detail, we begin with an overview of the drivers involved in the global labour migration process.

3.3 Conceptualizing Global Labour Migration

De Haas, Castles and Miller (2019) provide an overview of several core ideas around migration. They indicate how migration has spatial and temporal dimensions and increases with development, as aspirations and technologies in support of migration increase (De Haas et al. 2019). The actual per cent of international migrants as a share of total population has remained stable, at around 3 per cent, but aggregate numbers of migrants increase along with the growth of the global population. Overall, the authors of the *Age of Migration* argue that migration is an "intrinsic part of broader processes of development, globalization and social transformation rather than 'a problem to be solved'" (2019, p. 26). While this section addresses problems linked to the global migration of healthcare workers, the problem is not migration itself, but the wider global uneven development context within which it is occurring, and the context of inequitable reception that occurs in the labour markets where migrants arrive.

Various theories address the causes and impacts of migration and view the process through interlocking scales of analysis, including macro (global political-economy, including border control, and international relations); meso (migrant networks and intermediaries) and micro- (individual and family networks and linkages). Together these scales create an interactional system that influences more than just actual migrants; effectively migration is an intrinsic part of broader processes of development, social transformation and globalization. Traditional approaches to understanding migration processes have varied between functionalist explanations that see migration as part of a system of independent parts that adjust to reach and maintain some form of equilibrium (while arguably ignoring structural factors and homogenizing migrants and rationalizing their decision-making processes), and historical-structural approaches that are deterministic in terms of the excessive explanatory power allocated to structural factors while ignoring issues of agency. Between these two poles, more recent conceptualizations of migration emphasize multiple elements, including structures, migrant capabilities and aspirations to explain why some people migrate (De Haas et al. 2019).

Human migration can be understood as being an action in response to various drivers of migration, which can be structural as well as influenced by household or individual decisions. Multiple factors can cause migration to be initiated, and then subsequently perpetuated, and in combination these become the drivers of migration: "the term driver is reserved to describe the array of factors that may make up the external structural elements shaping the decision space for those considering migration" (Van Hear et al. 2018, p. 930). The conditions that determine the initiation of migration may be very different from those that contribute to its subsequent perpetuation, highlighting the fact that the drivers of migration will vary over space and time, even in what may ostensibly be seen as the same geographical pattern of migration (e.g., country A might initiate health worker migration from country B, but it is then subsequently perpetuated through migrant social networks). Van Hear et al. (2018) identify various kinds of drivers, including predisposing, proximate, precipitating and mediating. Predisposing drivers include economic, political and environmental disparities between locations that are reflective of global uneven development, as well as geographical factors, such as proximity between source and destination regions. Proximate drivers are more acute versions of the above disparities mentioned and include generalized conditions in sending or receiving regions such as economic growth, recession or political repression and environmental decline. Precipitating drivers are often attached to a specific event that becomes the trigger for the decision to migrate, such as a rise in unemployment or a specific natural disaster. While akin to predisposing drivers, proximate drivers can often be specifically identified in relation to the migrant's decision to migrate. Mediating factors can facilitate or constrain migration, such as transportation, information, "linguistic" flows, which can predispose migration as well as the recognition of qualifications, contributing to path dependency and personal (social) networks, as well as state-managed migration processes. Mediating factors can also include what has been called the migration infrastructure (Xiang & Lindquist 2014), and the existing culture of migration (which can be related to specific places as well as occupations, for example in the case of the "portable profession" of nursing (Kingma 2006) and its attraction to those interested in international migration opportunities (see Connell 2010b)).

In the next section we review drivers of migration with a specific focus on healthcare workers. Table 1 reviews these drivers of migration with specific examples relevant to healthcare workers. In predisposing, the drivers of migration include disparities in salary, working conditions, professional development, as well as some gendered disparities that influence the status of nursing in source regions, and how proximity influences migration patterns, for example, increased regional cross-border migration within Africa. Proximate drivers are generalized events that intensify these disparities, including the negative consequence of the HIV pandemic in Africa and the increased work pressures and risks it poses for health workers, or the outbreak of civil and political unrest. Precipitating drivers are more intense and immediate than proximate drivers. Mediating drivers facilitate migration, and include generalized improvements to transport, communication and personal/professional

Table 1 Drivers of migration related to healthcare worker migration from Van Hear et al. (2018)

Drivers of migration (Van Hear et al. 2018)	Description	Related to healthcare worker migration
Predisposing	Disparities – uneven development and geographical proximity	• Health worker salary gap between countries (George & Rhodes 2017). • Poor working conditions in source countries (Manyisa & van Aswegen 2017) and gender inequality related to source region-nursing (Bourgeault et al. 2021). • Changing migration patterns within Africa-proximity (Chikanda 2006).
Proximate	Events generating disparities	• HIV crisis in African countries (Awases et al. 2003) • Political conflict and physician emigration from Lebanon (Kronfol et al. 1992).
Precipitating	Specific event as trigger for the decision to migrate	• Political Crisis, Venezuela – medical worker outmigration (Daniels 2020), war in Serbia and physician outmigration (Wiskow 2006). • Syrian war and medical professional exit (Kallström et al. 2021).
Mediating	Facilitate or constrain migration including managed migration and migration infrastructure	• Japan's Economic Partnerships in nurse migration (Naiki 2015). • Medical recruiters (Connell & Stilwell 2006). • Filipino nursing labour agreements (Cabanda 2020). • Cuban physician agreements with South Africa (Hammett 2014).

networks, but also include the role of migration intermediaries and governments through bilateral agreements and other efforts to promote or support the migration of health workers.

The role of gender as a key variable in the migration process is important to consider in the case of healthcare workers, since globally, female healthcare workers constitute 70 per cent of the healthcare workforce which could increase up to 90 per cent if those working in the social care sector are included (social care includes those providing assistance with the activities of daily living in order to maintain independent and comfortable living) (Lotta et al. 2021). Anna Boucher (2007) has critically explored the role of gender in migration policy and suggested that "skill" definitions can reinforce the dichotomy between independent male and dependent female migrant categories. Our understanding of "skill" is informed by social stratifications based on class, gender, race and educational status, which creates "a hierarchy of migrant mobility within a hierarchy of nation-states" (Boucher 2007, p. 391). Women can face barriers in securing access to typically male-dominated occupational skills, and if their work is in traditionally feminized occupations, it is often devalued through its association with what are constructed as essentialized feminized traits, rather than skills and competencies. Moreover, occupational lists for the purpose of immigration sometimes exclude highly gendered professions such as nursing, and immigration policies more generally can be gendered and reproduce gender disadvantage in terms of devaluing women's unpaid social reproduction work (Boucher 2007).

3.3.1 Migrant Health Worker Integration and Regulation in Mainly Receiving Countries

While migration theories encourage us to attend to drivers of migration that span both agency and structural factors, the focus is primarily on understanding what is happening in the sending region, and those mediating factors that reflect an interactional relationship between sending and receiving countries. In addition to appreciating these features, we must also understand how migrant health workers then integrate into the national labour markets they migrate to, and this includes a better appreciation for the role of intermediaries and state agencies, and how intersectional factors such as gender, race, religion and national origin (among others) inform workplace integration and employment experiences in the destination country. The long-term integration process for internationally trained healthcare workers in higher-income countries has been evident since the expansion of national health systems post-1950s and 1960s (as explained in Section 1).

In the contemporary period, demand-driven and employer-initiated mobility of healthcare workers has increased, and the role of intermediaries in these contexts becomes important to understand. Migration intermediaries are "agents that intervene at various critical junctures to connect the migrant to the destination country labour market" (Van den Broek et al. 2016, p. 524). Van den Broek et al. (2016) argue that this migration infrastructure is usually seen as a black box, with intermediaries overlapping at a variety of stages in the migration process; operating in both origin and destination countries; and intervening at important junctures of the migration process, including negotiations over employment and living conditions. While relatively little is known about how labour market intermediaries shape the outcomes for skilled migrants and steer them into specific geographic, national and local labour markets, growing research has highlighted how the quality of information shared by intermediaries and other networks can channel workers into precarious sections of the labour market (Van den Broek & Groutsis 2017).

Shaffer et al. (2020) detail the nature of the recruitment industry for internationally trained health professionals in the USA, suggesting there are three main types: direct recruitment, placement and staffing. Direct recruitment is where health institutions hire international migrant health workers directly, typically covering related costs and providing employment. Placement recruiters handle immigration procedures and act as contractors who place workers with different health institutions where they are eventually employed. Staffing agencies act as both contractors and employers since they place the health worker with different institutions for short-term contracts but remain the employer of the worker. The staffing agency is considered the model that is most misaligned between the interests of the worker and the recruiter.

Chikanda (2022) argues that there has been a decline in the number of recruiters in the USA, which he sees as connected to the rise in ethical recruitment under the guidance of the WHO Code. Chikanda (2022) highlights the waxing and waning of flows between major supply and demand nations and considers the role of policies that curtail migration, such as visa retrogression, which limits the number of applicants from specific countries who can apply for a USA Green card. Visa retrogression and economic recession are two factors that have suppressed the recruitment of internationally educated nurses into the USA (Shaffer et al. 2020). Shaffer et al. (2020) also comment on consolidation among healthcare staffing agencies in the USA, suggesting that of the 15 largest in 2004, only 9 remained by 2020.

In addition to the WHO Code, other ethical frameworks include a domestic Alliance Code (Health Care Code for Ethical International Recruitment and Employment Practices). The first edition of this Alliance Code emerged in

2008 (predating the WHO code). The Alliance Code was developed by a multistakeholder group from across the USA healthcare sector, and they were tasked with informing stakeholders of the code, encouraging certification and overseeing compliance. Of the top five international health worker staffing agencies in the USA, two have been certified as ethical recruiters by the Alliance (Shaffer et al. 2020). A survey answered by over 1,000 foreign-educated health professionals found that the majority reported generally positive experiences with their recruiters, but some concerns with mistreatment, breaches in contract and fee conditions were evident. Overall, Shaffer et al. (2020) argue that improvements in the conditions of recruitment are necessary to provide more orderly and fair practices and to enhance the career progression and experience of international healthcare workers, which in turn promotes patient safety.

In addition to understanding why and how global migration occurs, and how mediating drivers such as recruiters operate, we also need to have some general understanding of how migrant labour is integrated into labour markets and workplaces. Labour immigration policies determine how immigrants that meet the needs of the destination country are admitted and what systems organize their entry into specific occupational sectors. National governments evaluate and respond to employers' claims that immigrants are needed to fill labour and skills shortages. Skills that are deemed necessary for specific jobs can be determined by employers to reflect their interests, including what they want to pay and other features they deem necessary (Ruhs & Anderson 2013). Employers might be selective, knowing that migrant workers will accept conditions and wage rates that non-migrants will not (and depending on possible recruitment paths, migrant intermediaries might reinforce this connection between migrant workers and lower-paid, poorer working conditions). Restrictive immigration status also makes it easier to retain immigrants in jobs with working conditions other people would not tolerate, especially if work visas are tied to employers. Immigrants might therefore be attractive as "high quality workers for low skilled jobs," and migrants might thereby provide a self-regulating and self-sustaining labour force because of the vulnerabilities they face due to these structural factors (Ruhs & Anderson 2013). Employers' decisions therefore occur within contextual constraints including labour market policy. For example, health and care workers may be needed and in demand, but a lack of national investment in the health sector results in conditions of low pay and insecure employment that domestic workers reject, and employers then use government immigration policy to recruit migrant health-care workers, who will accept these conditions, or are not aware of them until after they arrive.

In addition to these general conditions, regulated healthcare workers face other constraints that make labour market integration complicated, thereby increasing the need for effective support and relevant information from intermediaries and related agencies (Walton-Roberts 2020a). One of the complications of an internationalized circulation of health-care workers is the challenge of harmonization and credential recognition. These are complex since the professional standards of health-care workers typically demand, (a) pre-entry qualifications for interested students, (b) approval and accreditation from some type of quality council that is nationally/regionally recognized, (c) graduates generally need to satisfy licensure or registration exams to enter the profession and (d) these standards are typically geographically differentiated, whether within or between national units. Professional regulatory enforcement is complicated and expensive, and proactive methods to maintain quality are especially evident in self-regulatory professional associations or colleges that must justify and protect their right to self-regulate (Sweetman 2022). In the area of health care, this regulatory role is particularly acute, where professional misconduct is about matters of life and death. Professional associations do provide a solution to asymmetric information and high transaction costs (e.g., complex medical situations where the public has limited knowledge of procedures but must have trust in the system that identifies someone as a medical specialist in this area). Professional associations also risk monopoly power that can exact a social cost to society because they restrict the number of available professionals and increase the costs of their services (Sweetman et al. 2015).

Layered on top of national systems of regulation, there are examples of international frameworks to build comparable educational credentials for specific occupations, potentially leading to international mutual recognition for various professions. Examples include the Washington Accord for Engineers and the tuning or Bologna process in the European Higher Education Area (EHEA) (Kasuba & Ziliukas 2004; Walton-Roberts 2014). International quality assurance of medical facilities also includes guidance for verification of professional credentials. For example, the Joint Commission International (Pasternak & Chen 2016), whose mission is to improve the safety and quality of hospital care in the international community, recommends primary source verification be undertaken with all health professionals to protect the public interest. This provides an indication of the significance of the regulation of health professional standards, and the complexities introduced through the global migration of workers between different national regulatory jurisdictions (this will be taken up in more detail in Section 4).

3.3.2 Drivers and Consequences of Health Worker Migration in Mostly Sending Countries

Part of the inspiration for the creation of ethical recruitment codes in health worker migration has been the long-running concern that high-income nations, rather than invest in training their own health workers, have been poaching healthcare workers from lower-income nations causing significant damage to source country health systems in the process. However, past economic research has suggested that data are inconclusive regarding the extent to which skilled worker outmigration negatively affects the source country, including healthcare systems, suggesting that there may be several benefits associated with skilled migration that must be assessed alongside potentially negative consequences (Gibson & McKenzie 2011, Docquier & Rapoport 2012). These benefits include better living and working conditions and wages, the development of new skills and competencies, as well as the development potential of migrant remittances sent back to the sending region. The WHO's Global Strategy on Human Resources for Health: Workforce 2030 outlines the policies needed to support the SDGs (WHO 2016b). Based on the calculation of minimum thresholds of health workers needed to meet UHC and SDGs, the WHO determined an SDG index threshold of 4.45 doctors, nurses and midwives per 1,000 population. Using this SDG index, the global shortage of health workers by 2030 was calculated to be 14.5 million. In addressing this potential shortage, the WHO advocates for improved recruitment, training and retention of health workers, and adoption of more diverse and sustainable skills mix focused on primary health care, together, with efforts to increase productivity and performance. High-income nations face challenges in terms of the aging profile of their populations and attaining health worker sustainability demands improved workforce planning. This includes addressing market failures that contribute to health worker maldistribution, improving retention and lowering their dependence on internationally recruited health workers (Buchan et al. 2019).

Countries that are primarily migrant source regions for health workers face all the challenges outlined in the drivers of migration (Table 1). This includes employment conditions that offer lower income, poorer working conditions and weaker career progression conditions relative to other countries. While employment income and working conditions are significant drivers for health worker migration, contextual factors are important to examine. In a comparative study of source country perspectives of health worker migration, including Jamaica, South Africa, India and the Philippines, various nuances and transformations in health worker outmigration patterns were revealed. In Jamaica, Tomblin-Murphy et al. (2016) found that despite a long tradition of health worker outmigration, the process was poorly monitored and understood, and regardless of national and international policy efforts to address health worker migration, the process remained a systematic response to differences in the living and working conditions between Jamaica and key destination countries. In India evidence of a lack of data on health worker migration was also evident (Walton-Roberts et al. 2017b), and policymakers' views of the outmigration of health-care workers were ambivalent, since state and national government officials saw the beneficial contributions made by international migration. Wider concerns regarding the conditions of training and career progression were also seen as contributing to some of the shortages and maldistribution of health workers across India, suggesting that migration was only one compounding factor among many others in terms of managing health worker training, retention and distribution (Walton-Roberts et al. 2017b). In the Philippines, a long-term structural orientation to health worker outmigration has commercialized education systems to the extent that the number of nurses trained significantly exceeds domestic employment capacities. As such without wider economic development and health system investment to provide better incentives for health workers, nurses will not be able to find viable employment options in the Philippines. There are also complex social costs of migration borne by migrants and their families that have accompanied the outward orientation of health worker training (Castro-Palaganas et al. 2017). The four country studies also revealed the importance of analyzing changes in health worker migration patterns over time. For example, the South African research team (Labonté et al. 2015) found that the previously high rates of outmigration of skilled health workers have been addressed by several policies to improve the conditions of work for health professionals in South Africa. This, combined with fluctuations in demand, resulted in a reduction of outmigration. In its place higher rates of migration for the purposes of skill/career development were evident, and as a result, permanent outmigration has reduced as a major policy concern for the country.

The study of source countries for health worker migration found that policymakers interviewed for the research were relatively uninformed about the WHO Code on the international recruitment of health workers, and reference to it was generally absent in policy documents (Bourgeault et al. 2016). International organizations were more aware of the Code, but also aware of its lack of impact on health worker migration. There was a sense that better coordination between different ministries (trade and health) was needed, together with deeper cooperation on migration policy and development, including bilateral agreements. The source country perspectives of health worker migration project revealed the value of engaging with country-specific analysis of health worker migration.

The research revealed differences in terms of the scope of migration for different occupations, the perspectives of government and other stakeholders, and the different consequences (negative and positive) of international health worker migration. The country-specific studies reveal nuances in terms of how health worker migration is perceived, but also the widespread lack of awareness and application of the WHO Code on the international recruitment of health-care workers. Other factors emerging include the lack of connection between concerned ministries of trade and health in sending countries, and the need to focus on collaboration between countries to find solutions to manage the global mobility of this resource. This type of collaboration includes the design and use of bilateral agreements that can serve the needs of migrants and both the sending and receiving countries.

The source country perspective studies revealed a diversity of policy perspectives and consequences related to health worker migration for source countries. The value of this type of comparative research is that it can assist us to understand how health worker training systems might be distorted by the intensity of the orientation of training systems to global opportunities. For example, in both the Philippines and India there have been distortions in the nursing education and training system, which have an impact on quality, cost, employment and the overall health systems in sending states (Brush & Sochalski 2007; Walton-Roberts 2015a). Multiple actors are involved in this process, leading to outcomes that can contribute to the continuous reproduction of health worker migration systems that are orientated to international, not domestic, markets. This can be because the costs of privatized education outstrip the possible salaries that can be earnt domestically, practically invoking migration as a necessary fiscal response. In the case of the Philippines, there is also concern that the distortions created by outmigration demand create internal opportunities for the exploitation of newly graduated nurses by demanding they volunteer in hospitals to gain the skills needed to enter migration networks (Ortiga 2018a). The overall effect of these and other distortions in training because of international migration pose deep challenges to meeting the SDGs (Thompson & Walton-Roberts 2019).

More recent research on the approach of source countries reveals how some states are recognizing the benefits of health worker mobility and exploring how to benefit from it. Efendi et al. (2021) examine Indonesian policymakers and stakeholders' views on the management of overseas migration of Indonesian nurses. The article notes an excess of nurses in Indonesia and increased demand for nurses globally has resulted in many nurses migrating out of Indonesia. The authors conclude policies and communication between stakeholders need to be strengthened, and challenges must be addressed throughout the process of international migration, including in the pre-migration, migration and post-migration stages. The authors discuss solutions to address the issue through four themes; moving towards global market orientation, addressing challenges in international nurse migration, strengthening coordination among stake-holders and making the most of opportunities to "make Indonesian nurses more competitive and adaptive in global market" (Efendi 2021, p. 3285). Efendi et al.'s (2021) approach highlights how states might consider how their demographic profile offers them a competitive advantage if they can develop effective training systems to mass produce or oversupply nurse gradu-ates and, in the process, service international markets. These issues are particu-larly important for Asia, a key source region for migrant nurses (Hawthorne 2015), where countries such as India, Vietnam and the Philippines, are, to different degrees, utilizing the private sector to produce nurses explicitly for global export to countries such as Canada, Germany and Singapore (Clemens 2015; Walton-Roberts 2015a; Masselink & Lee 2010; Hillman et al. 2022). The risk of such orientation, however, is the perpetuation of the outmigration of health workers, without an effective domestic internal development agenda to accompany it. In the absence of domestic development, the outmigration process becomes a never-ending self-perpetuating cycle of training for export, with only partial returns accrued to the sending nation (Castro-Palaganas et al. 2017; Cabanda 2020).

To intervene in this cycle, researchers must also ask what might bring healthcare workers back. Alameddine et al. (2019) examine what might encourage Lebanese emigrant nurses back to their country to practice nursing. Solutions include better economic security, increased education and continuous professional development. This article is noteworthy for its comparative evaluation of nurses settled in Gulf and non-Gulf states regarding their intention to return to practice in Lebanon. The focus on what policy approaches might be effective in attracting nurses to return has relevance to other national contexts. The article also explored broader gender dynamics associated with the international migration of nurses, particularly understanding contextual differences regarding what might motivate male nurses to return.

3.3.3 Transit Countries and the Dynamics of Migration Decision Making

The increasing complexity of migration pathways and the spatially differenti-ated regimes of skill that govern them, create contexts that increase the tempor-ariness of the migration experience as migrants engage in two-step, circular, seasonal and intermittent mobility. Empirical research on migration has tended to underplay the scope and importance of these multiple migrations (Paul & Yeoh 2021), which can entail several geographical and/or visa status experiences (Percot 2006; Hawthorne 2010). For skilled workers such as healthcare workers, transit migration also allows for career development and skill building, which can eventually support onward migration to higher-income nations offering better living and working conditions (Percot 2006). Work in the USA by Artuc and Ozden (2018) found that 9 per cent of migrant arrivals between 2001 and 2012 were living in a country other than their birthplace before arriving in the USA, and this increases to 14 per cent for those with tertiary education. Artuc and Ozden (2018, p. 308) use the term "transit migration" "to describe any migrant who lives in a foreign country before moving to a second foreign country." They found most transit migrants to the USA had a tertiary education and were born in high-income European and some African and East Asian nations. The authors argue that current migration stock and flow data examine migration decision-making through a bilateral lens, assuming decision-making occurs in terms of the differences between a sending and receiving context, whereas evidence suggests migration processes and trajectories may be more complex than this, involving multiple migration stages framed by decisions about costs, opportunities and barriers. Transit routes can open opportunities for onward migration that might not be possible directly from the origin country, such as migration to countries on the periphery of the EU in hope of later gaining EU access. Transit routes might also feed migrants into onward movement because restrictive immigration policies might limit the length of time one can reside there and the rights one can access (such as the ability to claim permanent residence and sponsor family members to join). Artuc and Ozden (2018) create a dynamic structural model that captures sequential and transit migration patterns and creates an option value of a location based on the opportunities it offers for subsequent migration (in this case to the USA). These can be dynamic in that the option value of a location will change as the ease of potential movement from that location to another changes (consider the departure of the UK from the EU). Other factors that inform the model are the friction of distance (high-skilled immigrants are less affected by distance than low-skilled) and language commonality (which decreases migration costs). The authors determine that transit migration is more common among high-skilled migrants, including those living in OECD nations, and those from Africa and the Middle East. In calculating the presence of transit migration, the authors were limited to focusing on the USA since this is where they could access relevant data, but their findings indicate the importance of understanding location option values in terms of the opportunities for onward migration and how policy changes that alter or limit migration have externalities associated with them that can affect neighbouring states.

In terms of health professional migration, especially for key source countries such as India and the Philippines, how systems of skilled migration co-evolve with the policy contexts of receiving states can be illustrated in Gulf Co-operation Council (GCC) countries, as well as Asian health nodes such as Singapore and Malaysia. In these cases, healthcare workers are in demand to provide health services to local populations, in addition to servicing the growing demands of medical tourism aligned to growing south-south regional associations, such as ASEAN or Southern Africa Development Community (SADC) health service centers (Ormond 2020). The degree of migrant rights offered in these destination markets varies and contributes to their positioning as transit rather than permanent sites of settlement. The significance of transit routes is clear for skilled migrants who rely on intermediaries. Van den Broek et al. (2016) suggest that intermediaries may charge different fee rates based on the migrant source and destination country (seen in the case of fees for nurse migrants) resulting in a segmented cost structure, but also potentially leading to misinformation regarding contracts and working conditions for applicants. Van den Broek et al. (2016) suggest that intermediaries provide the poorest information and service in areas where demand is high (this is generally in lower-income source nations). The demand pressure and market potential of these systems might result in migrants being sent to underperforming areas of the labour market, which leads to the reproduction of ethnic and gender stereotyping, potentially devaluing the human capital these migrants embody intensifying their precarity (Van den Broek & Groutsis 2017) and directing migrants to locations that have lower "option values" in terms of onward migrant opportunities (cf Artuc & Ozden 2018). This can arguably be seen in the migration of nurses from India to GCC countries, where public concern regarding fraud and misrepresentation by intermediaries has caused the Government of India to intervene in the migration process by imposing controls on nurses who intend to migrate (Varghese 2020). This is achieved by channelling migration through six government-approved intermediaries and encouraging receiving countries to work with the Indian government's e-Migrate platform to create postings that can then be monitored. This type of state policy control represents a form of gendered migration governance that focuses on controlling migration without attending to improving the working conditions and status of the nursing profession in the source or destination markets (Walton-Roberts et al., 2022). Despite these problems, this migration route remains attractive (whether undertaken through or outside of state-regulated channels) in part because Indian trained nurses have used GCC countries as a stepping-stone to subsequent sites of permanent settlement such as Ireland, the UK, Canada and the USA (Percot 2006).

Another example of a location with a high option value in terms of onward migration is Singapore. Research on migration from the Philippines to Singapore has termed this model a "bus stop" where workers wait for a specific opportunity or 'bus' to take them to the next stop (Walton-Roberts 2021). The term emerges from an interview with a Singapore-based immigration consultant who explained how skilled temporary migrant workers in Singapore use the work experience they have gained in Singapore to advance their migration journey toward preferable destinations that offer permanent residence. Foreign-trained nurses are integral to the healthcare system in Singapore (Yeoh & Huang 2014, 2015), but their options for permanent settlement are highly restrictive and their labour market experiences are marked by highly stratified experiences of workplace integration that diminishes their professional identity and status (Amrith 2017). This means that nurses occupy an ambiguous position between skilled and unskilled labour (Choi & Lyons 2012). Singapore's care migration context represents a "liberal private market approach" where care has been commoditized and the state provides incentives for families to purchase elder and childcare through temporary migration (Peng 2018). The state tightly controls this migration regime maintaining it as a temporary model managed through networks of placement agencies (Hillman et al. 2022). As a result, Singapore hires autonomous and self-funded migrants through various recruitment networks, which pose typical challenges of misrepresentation (Van den Broek et al. 2016). Singapore, as a member of ASEAN, is also part of the region-wide Mutual Recognition Agreement (MRA) scheme, which includes the occupation of nursing, but this agreement has led to relatively little change on the ground in terms of the mobility of nurses through the region, since they still must meet nationally determined occupational criteria (Te et al. 2018). The options for permanent residence for migrant nurses have also been constrained since the "watershed" election of 2011, which communicated national dissatisfaction with increased migration into the city-state (Yeoh & Lam 2016).

These migration examples illustrate the point made by Artuc and Ozden (2018) regarding transit route dynamics, and how the option values of these locations change in relation to the potential onward migration routes possible. Singapore's option value is reflected in the opportunities it provides for work experience and the possibility of "hopping on the bus" to subsequent locations with higher option values. Singapore is not an attractive long-term settlement option due to limited rights for migrants (Amrith 2017). GCC nations offer a similar context, where citizenship rights are negligible for most migrants and constrained even for highly skilled physicians and other skilled workers (Walton-Roberts & Khadria 2023).

3.4 Foreign Trained versus Foreign Born Healthcare Workers

This final section reflects on one more complexity related to the migration and mobility of healthcare workers. So far this section has defined health worker migrants as those who have secured most of their training in their country of birth and have then engaged in forms of migration that may include career development as well as employment but are effectively moving away from their country of birth. Health workforce data collected by international agencies such as OECD or WHO includes data on "foreign trained" as opposed to foreign born. Those workers who are foreign trained can include circuits of health and medical education exchanges between countries including international institutional exchanges and training agreements. This global training of healthcare workers can be seen in terms of specialized training, calls for transnational medical education to treat diverse patients and manage cultural differences between care provider and patient (Koehn 2006), to creating global or post-colonial understandings of health (Harden 2006; Bleakley et al. 2008). "Foreign trained" health workers therefore present a further layer of complexity in terms of understanding who is making the investment in training these health workers, where is this training occurring, and where these workers finally provide service. We are also witnessing increasingly geographically complex training pathways that include global health education as part of the national curriculum (Bandyopadhyay et al. 2020), and offshore medical education being pursued in response to national rationing of government-funded health training (Morgan et al. 2018). This section considers the presence of foreign-trained health workers based on data from the WHO's National Health Accounts (WHO 2018). This allows us to understand the comparative dependence national health systems have on internationally trained workers. In some cases, this includes reliance on migrant workers, but in some cases it includes national citizens who have gained some of their training overseas. Understanding the level of dependency different countries have on international training is relevant to health workforce self-sufficiency and the pursuit of UHC.

To support the pursuit of UHC and to meet the Global Strategy on human resources for health 2030, the 69th WHA passed the resolution for member states to consolidate data on human resources for health and implement national health workforce accounts. The WHO National Health Workforce Accounts (NHWA) is a system through which countries can share their health workforce data and work towards improvements in the availability, quality and use of such data to reach the SDGs and UHC. Countries have access to web platforms to upload data. Data is also available through the NHWA data portal (https://apps.who.int/nhwaportal/Home/Index) providing country profiles, occupational profiles and key statistics. The platform also includes data queries, including "place of training" where "foreign trained" can be identified for all countries and various health professions.

Table 2 includes data from the NHWA portal for those countries that have submitted data where they indicate over 50 per cent of health occupations have received their training abroad. The data in the portal are provided by member states, and NHWA metadata includes the following statement. "Due to the differences in data sources, considerable variability remains across countries in the coverage, periodicity, quality, and completeness of the original data. Therefore, we invite users to be cautious when deriving interpretations from international comparisons." The first observation is the surprising number and range of member states indicating that 100 per cent of doctors, nurses or midwives are foreign trained. This includes EU members such as Cyprus and Hungary, where training capacity and intra-EU mobility may frame the nature of health professional training, resulting in a large per cent of domestic students securing their education (or parts thereof) in other EU countries before returning to their country to practice. The second observation is that there are several small island states, such as Maldives, San Tome and Principe, Seychelles, Tonga, Tuvalu and Nuie, listed where training capacity is limited and health professionals receive their education overseas through Pacific and other health partnerships. Third, there are a few states where Official development assistance is provided in the form of health training partnerships. This includes Zambia's partnership with China, which sees Zambian physicians trained in China and Chinese technical experts working in Zambia, and several cases where Cuban medical assistance is provided through the provision of health training, including, Kiribati, Timor-Leste and Namibia. Fourth, we see countries from the GCC, where domestic health education and the promotion of such employment for domestic populations have only recently developed, and these countries have come to depend on a large immigrant health workforce (Ennis & Walton-Roberts 2018). Finally, it is worth pointing out that three countries – Kiribati, Micronesia and Chad – are included in this table and listed on the WHO's critical shortage list for healthcare workers. This safeguard list is generated by the WHO and includes countries with the most pressing UHC-related health workforce needs. These nations are prioritized for health personnel development and health system–related support; and need to be provided with safeguards that discourage active international recruitment of health personnel. The inclusion of these three countries in this table indicates how dependent some small island states and low-income nations are on bringing in internationally trained workers and/or relying upon international partners for health worker training to meet their healthcare needs.

Table 2 Place of training "foreign trained," all occupations, all countries WHO NHWA data portal.

Country	Year	MD., N. or MW.	Foreign Trained Value (%)	Context	Reference(s)
Belize	2017	MD	100.00	• No medical training facility	Directorate General for Foreign Trade 2021
Bhutan	2020	MD	90.60	• Limited medical education training capacity • Students are trained in India, Bangladesh, Sri Lanka, Thailand, Myanmar or Nepal	Tobgay et al. 2011
Brunei Darussalam	2018	MD	100.00	• Few local training options • Import many of their healthcare workers	Connell 2010b
Chad[a]	2020	MD	63.80	• Limited training capacity • Chadian students receive scholarships from other francophone or Arab countries • Medical experts trained in France and returned to Chad	Chad – Higher Education, n.d.; • Sufi 2013

Country	Year		%		Reference
Cyprus	2017	MD	100.00	• No medical faculties existed in Cyprus universities • First graduated from universities in Cyprus in 2019	Eurostat Health Care Staff 2021
Guyana	2019	MD	100.00	• Political instability, no option for further training • Greater income abroad, international partners for education	Persaud et al. 2017
Hungary	2020	N	100.00	• Only in 2000s did a higher education option become available • Need greater workforce planning	Betelhem et al. 2017
	2020	MW	100.00	• Higher wages in destination • Many leave the profession	Boros et al. 2022
	2020	MD	100.00	• Economic crisis, politics push to migrate	Varga 2017
Israel	2020	MD	57.80	• Limited medical training capacity in Israel • Students train overseas	Linder 2021
Jordan	2017	MD	70.00	• Graduates leave the country to seek specialty and subspecialty education and training abroad	Abdel-Razeq et al. 2020

Table 2 (cont.)

Country	Year	MD, N. or MW.	Foreign Trained Value (%)	Context	Reference(s)
Kiribati[a]	2014	MD	100.00	• Income and employment conditions are better elsewhere	Connell 2010b
Kuwait	2020	MD	50.00	• Only one medical training facility exists in the country • Many were sent to Canada, UK or USA for training • Heavy reliance on expatriate healthcare workers	Al-Jarallah et al. 2010; WHO 2017c
	2020	N	50.00	• No graduate nursing programs available as of 2010 • Socio-cultural factors and unfavourable working conditions, thus many migrate Heavy reliance on expatriate healthcare workers	
Maldives	2018	MD	100.00	• High reliance on expatriate health professionals	Tangcharoensathien et al. 2018

Country	Year	Type	%	Notes	Source
Micronesia[a] (Federated States of)	2014	MD	100.00	• Do not have their own training institutions	Itaki 2020
Monaco	2016	N	100.00	• Many study in France	WHO 2020c
	2016	MD	100.00	• No medical facility at university	WHO 2020c
Namibia	2017	MD	96.30	• Inadequate local training capacity. • Doctors had to travel abroad to South Africa, Russia, Cuba, Algeria and China to be educated	Fihlani 2016; McQuide et al. 2013
Niue	2018	N	94.40	• Nurses train overseas • Fly in fly out medical care	Sheel & Rendell 2022
Oman	2017	MD	70.50%	• Historical reliance on migrant health workers	Ghosh 2019
	2017	MW	52.50%		
	2017	N	51.80		
Palau	2020	N	100.00	• Employ many Fijians • Many nurses go abroad for better salary	Bureau of International Organization Affairs & Office of United Nations Political Affairs 1989; Connell 2010b
	2020	MW	100.00	• Employ many Fijians • Many go abroad for training due to lack of facilities	Connell 2010b
	2020	MD	100.00	• Employ many Fijians • Many go abroad for training due to limited facilities	Pierantozzi 2005; Connell 2010b

Table 2 (cont.)

Country	Year	MD., N. or MW.	Foreign Trained Value (%)	Context	Reference(s)
Poland	2018	N	100.00	• Many work elsewhere in the EU • Significant portion of nursing graduates are not entering the profession • Long process to become a nurse in Poland	Main 2020
Qatar	2018	MW	100.00	• Lack of training and education in country • Partnerships with other nations provide training	Al-Harahsheh et al. 2020
Saint Lucia	2017	MD	91.40	• Lack of national medical schools • Five medical universities but most are international student driven	Sammie 2014; IFEM 2020

Country	Year		%	Notes	References
São Tomé and Príncipe	2019	N	100.00	• Few professional and financial opportunities	CMAJ 2010
	2019	MD	100.00	• Natives who go abroad for medical training often opt not to return home to practise • No medical schools	Fronteira et al. 2014
Saudi Arabia	2017	MD	73.20	• Many nurses are from China and Indonesia, foreign-trained nurses have been readily available • Many continue to study abroad • High turnover rates • Lack of hospitals under medical colleges, reliance on foreign doctors	Alluhidan et al. 2020; Connell 2010b; Al-Hanawi et al. 2019; Saudi Gazette 2018; Zawawi & Al-Rashed 2020
	2017	N	77.10		
Seychelles	2018	MD	100.00	• No medical program at their one university • Lack of additional training	Karapetyan 2019
	2018	MW	100.00	• Only one medical training facility exists in the country • Many were sent to Canada, UK or USA for training	Pope 2018; Pointe 2020

Table 2 (cont.)

Country	Year	MD., N. or MW.	Foreign Trained Value (%)	Context	Reference(s)
Thailand	2019	N	100.00	• Country has not developed policy and systematic management of outmigration	Tangcharoensathien et al. 2018
	2019	MD	100.00	• Many have received their credentials overseas in the USA or UK	Kennedy Center For International Studies 2022
Timor-Leste	2020	MD	100.00	• Do not own training program • Cuban-Timorese doctor-training program initiated by Fidel Castro (the Cuban medical brigade)	Hodal 2012
Tonga	2020	MD	100.00	• All doctors are trained overseas • Due to income incentives and better working conditions	Brown & Connell 2004; Connell 2010b
Tuvalu	2018	N	100.00	• No training facilities • Must go abroad to complete studies	Connell 2010b

Zambia	2018	MD	99.70	• Many were trained at Chinese, Russian or Ukraine universities	Luska Times 2018
	2018	N	99.40	• Better pay overseas • Many work in the UK	Kline 2003, Nolan 2022

[a] Countries on shortage and safeguard list

[b] MD, Medical Doctor; MW, Midwifery Personnel; N, Nursing Personnel

Note: Only those countries with values above 50 per cent are listed. Countries in red are on the WHO critical shortage list. Listing is alphabetical.

Attending to the deeper complexities of health worker migration through analysis of the degree of foreign training health workers rely on reveals the structural
challenges of providing adequate training capacity, as well as retaining workers
once they have been trained. It is also clear from some of the European examples
that health worker mobility can be ingrained in the professional development
process and is not necessarily indicative of weaknesses in training systems, but
reflective of deeper regional integration and labour mobility processes.

3.5 Conclusion

We have reviewed the importance of healthcare workers to health systems and
considered how the international mobility and integration of such workers are
integral to the operation and resilience of health systems globally. To understand
migration and mobility of healthcare workers more deeply, the different drivers of
migration were examined and related specifically to healthcare workers. The
overarching frameworks used to conceptualize international migration include
the idea of a series of push or pull factors that frame the driving forces that propel
migratory interest. Added to this traditional approach to international migration is
the role of network factors (intermediaries) that connect between sites, these
include stakeholders who might promote and market mobility to potential
migrants. Moving from the drivers predominately in the sending state, we then
turned to consider labour market integration and the types of barriers health
professionals face, particularly in terms of credential recognition and licensing.
The non-recognition or devaluation of foreign credentials are significant barriers
for migrants, and the cumulative effects they have on healthcare systems, workplace integration, domestic economies, economic and social development, and
health workers and patient care, play an important role in unsettling health care.
Migration contexts were examined in each of the sending, receiving and transit
contexts while appreciating countries can function as all three of these simultaneously. To further illustrate the diversity and complexity of health worker mobility, we examined the case of healthcare workers who are "foreign trained" but not
necessarily migrants. Such mobility reflects an increasing internationalization of
health professional training, but also the type of global health solidarity and
development initiatives that have emerged to assist countries facing critical health
worker shortages and face challenges to meet the SDGs and UHC goals.

The international mobility of health workers is increasingly dynamic and complex, with countries simultaneously positioned as sites of sending, receiving and
transit migration. In addition, more complex patterns of mobility are evident in
terms of spatial (the direction of migration pathways), temporal (short, long term
and circular form of migration associated with work as well as training and career

progression) as well as institutional dimensions (where health worker mobility is organized through state-to-state development initiatives).

All nations need to address the challenges of securing the necessary numbers, skill mix and distribution of healthcare workers to meet the SDGs and secure UHC. The COVID-19 pandemic has reaffirmed the importance of addressing health system resilience and building systems that can be enabled to meet surge demands. In the past health systems were seen as a cost for national finances, but healthcare needs to be seen as an investment in population health and as an important sector of the economy itself. The long-term returns from enhanced health investment and improved employment conditions for the sizable labour force involved in health and care services are driving a global agenda that has been escalated by the COVID-19 pandemic.

4 International Policy Responses to Health Worker Mobilities

4.1 Introduction

We have explored the centrality of healthcare workers to the effective provision of health and care services, and how the distorted distribution of those workers reflects global uneven development and poses a challenge to meeting the aspirational goals of the SDGs and UHC. The international migration and recruitment of trained healthcare workers have traditionally posed a significant concern regarding the development of middle- and low-income nations, particularly African countries, and small Island states. It is also a specifically gendered concern, since 70 per cent of health and care workers are women, and the working conditions they face, whether in their birth countries or elsewhere, are of significant relevance to wider development goals. The global perspective of health worker distribution and mobility is framed through the convergence of several international instruments. The aspirational goals of the SDGs place health and gender as a cross-cutting factor instrumental to all facets of the goals.

The WHO has calculated a threshold of healthcare workers needed to meet the SDGs and UHC based on 12 key population health indicators weighted according to the global burden of disease (WHO 2016b). The results allow for the calculation of an SDG index threshold of 4.45 doctors, nurses and midwives per 1,000 population (44.5 per 10,000) which represents the minimum density needed. Based on this threshold, the current and projected shortages of healthcare workers were calculated at 17.4 million in 2013 (including 2.6 million doctors and 9 million nurses and midwives). The shortage is projected to remain at around 14.5 million in 2030, but more recent estimates posted by the WHO suggest the shortage by 2030 is now 10 million. The global maldistribution of healthcare workers is a perpetual development concern, but various demographic and epidemiological changes (aging and the rise on non-communicable diseases) and the consequences of the COVID-19 pandemic, have exposed the lack of resiliency in middle- and high-income nation's health systems, as well as the already underdeveloped health systems in low-income nations. These combined pressures will now intensify demands on health systems, and potentially reignite international health worker recruitment demands as health systems everywhere attempt to respond to shortages (Buchan et al. 2022).

Figures 4 and 5, map the distribution and density of doctors and nursing and midwifery personnel globally in terms of their numbers per 10,000 population. Considering the SDG threshold of 44.5 health workers (doctors, nurses and allied health workers) per 10,000, densities below this threshold are evident in low- and middle-income nations, especially across Africa, Asia and parts of Latin America. The distribution of healthcare workers is highly unequal globally, thus posing a challenge to meeting various goals, including the SDGs and UHC.

Table 3 presents similar information regarding health workforce density as of 2013 and projected to 2030, as well as the projected shortages based on the SDG threshold (WHO 2016a). It is evident that Southeast Asia and Africa are forecast to face the greatest shortages of health workers by 2030, and that Africa is the one WHO region that remains below the SDG threshold based on the projected figures for 2030.

Recognizing the significance of healthcare workers to the effective provision of health services, the international mobility of this type of worker garners specific interest when it represents a draining of human health resources from low-income to high-income nations. Addressing this issue has been the focus of numerous efforts at the level of international organizations, where the inherently global and transnational nature of international migration is best addressed as a policy issue relevant to the right to health and transnational social justice issues (Connell & Buchan 2011; Yeates & Pillinger 2019). Trained healthcare worker migrants are subject to a voluntary global code of governance, the WHO's Global Code of Practice on the International Recruitment of Health Personnel (WHO 2010b). The goal of the Code is to reduce the active recruitment of health workers from countries facing critical shortages, and for high-income receiving nations to commit to achieving health worker self-sufficiency.

4.2 The Evolution of Codes on International Health Worker Migration and Recruitment

The evolution of voluntary codes of practice on the international recruitment of healthcare workers is illustrated in Figure 6. This evolution includes several precursor agreements to the 2010 WHO Code, including global agreements that

Medical doctors (per 10,000)

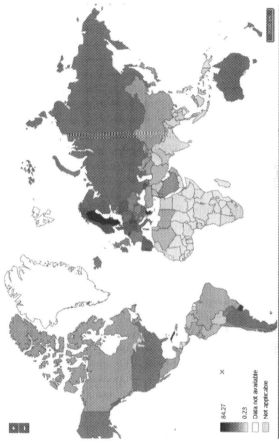

Figure 4 Doctors per 10,000 population, latest available

dates (source WHO Global Health Observatory www.who.int/data/gho/data/themes/topics/health-workforce).

Nursing and midwifery personnel (per 10,000)

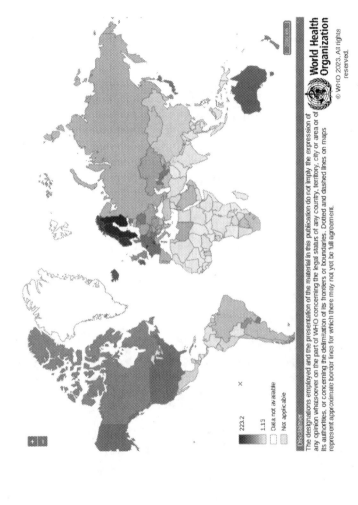

Figure 5 Nursing and midwifery personnel per 10,000 population, latest available

dates (source WHO Global Health Observatory www.who.int/data/gho/data/themes/topics/health-workforce).

Table 3 Healthcare worker density, 2030 forecast and shortages (WHO 2016a).

World Region	Health workers per 1,000 population 2013 (WHO 2016a)	Health workers per 1,000 population forecast by 2030 (in millions) (WHO 2016a)	Health worker shortages by 2030 based on SDG index threshold of 4.45 workers per 1,000 (in millions)
Africa	1.9	3.1	6.1
Americas	9.4	14.0	0.6
Eastern Mediterranean	3.1	5.3	1.7
Europe	12.7	16.8	0.1
Southeast Asia	6.2	10.9	4.7
Western Pacific	10.3	17.3	1.4

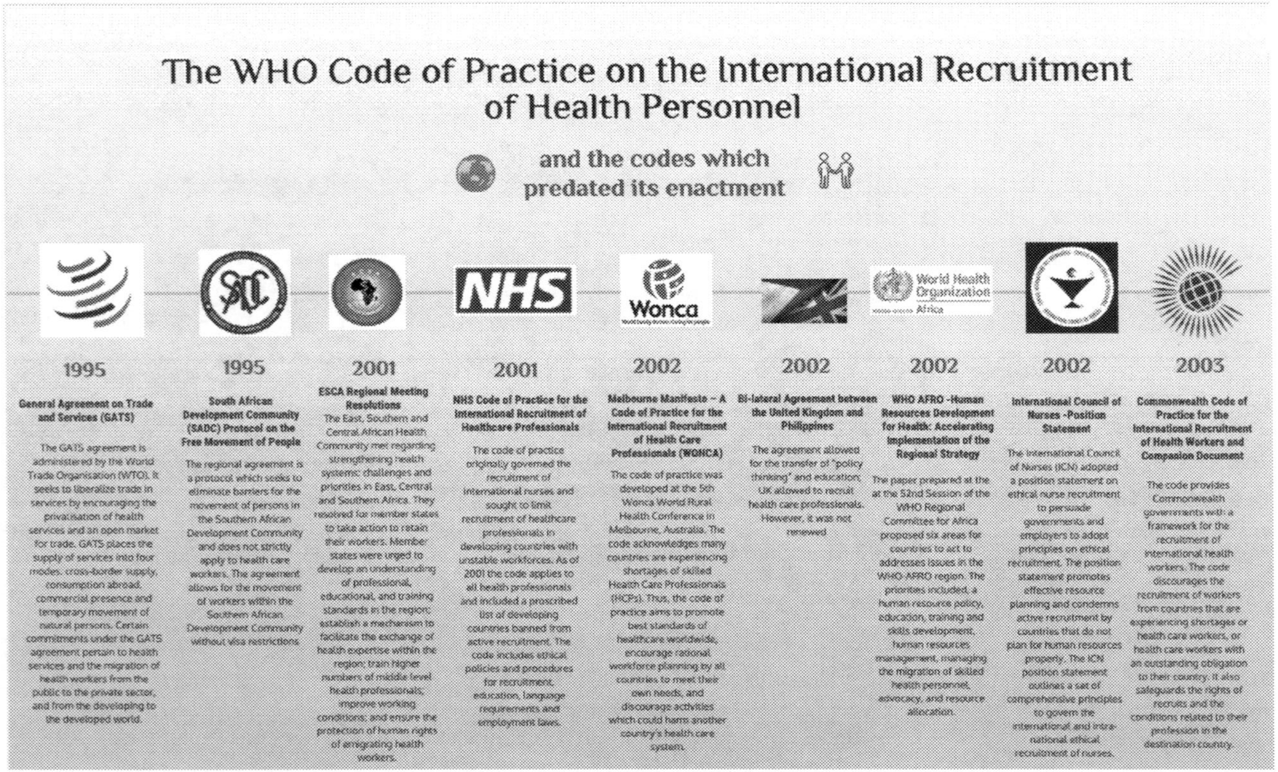

Figure 6 Evolution of voluntary codes 1995–2010 (graphic by Samantha Zani).

2003

Memorandum of Understanding between South Africa and United Kingdom

The bilateral agreement sought to address the recruitment, exchange, and development of health care workers between the UK and South Africa since South Africa is a primary source country of workers for the UK. It was signed for a 5-year period and renewed in 2006 for another 5 years to facilitate an exchange of health care workers and expertise.

2003

World Medical Associations statement on Ethical Guidelines for the International Recruitment of Physicians

The statement recognises the physician's valid reasons for migrating to developed countries but also recognises the impact that movement has on developing source countries. The guidelines are framed by three ethical principles: justice, co-operation, and autonomy. The WMA recommendations urge countries to ensure proper human resource planning and to not rely on immigration for health professionals.

NEPAD
TRANSFORMING AFRICA

2003

NEPAD Health Strategy

The strategy seeks to 'establish or strengthen health systems and services so they can provide effective and equitable health care'. NEPAD identifies six sectors as priorities for achieving the goals of the health strategy, a major priority is human resources development, which is aimed at reversing the brain drain. The health strategy focuses on both retention and migration strategies.

2004

Memorandum of Understanding between Namibia and Kenya on Technical Cooperation in Health

The memorandum provides guidelines for temporary (unidirectional) movement of health workers from Kenya to Namibia upon the request of Namibia. It was formed as result of Kenya's inability to fully employ its health workers under terms of an IMF agreement.

2004

Migration Dialogue for Southern Africa

The Migration Dialogue for Southern Africa was formed to facilitate open dialogue and cooperation on migration policy issues within the Southern African Development Community (SADC). Recommendations regarding the migration of health personnel were considered by governments, international agencies, and civil society organisations. Strategies to retain health care workers, enhance training, implement monitoring and evaluation of systemic effectiveness, government engagement and migration management were discussed.

2004

World Health Assembly Resolution 57.19

Resolution 57.19 addresses international migration of health personnel as a challenge for health systems in developing countries. The resolution proposes member states develop strategies to mitigate adverse affects of migration of health personnel and minimize negative impact on health systems.

LONDON DECLARATION
Patients for Patient Safety
WHO Patient Safety

2005

London Declaration

The British Medical Association (BMA) convened an international global health workforce conference in association with the commonwealth to formulate and endorse new principles on the migration of health workers, commonly referred to as the London Declaration. They recognised the migration of health workers from developing to developed countries has a deleterious impact on the health-care workforce of developing countries and is a growing concern for developing countries.

www.southafrica.info

2006

South Africa Department of Health Policy on Recruitment, Employment and Support of Foreign Health Professionals and Recruitment of Foreign Health Professional Guidelines

The policy approved by The National Department of Health in South Africa regulates the recruitment, employment, migration, and support of foreign health professionals' residency status in South Africa. It outlines the legal rights of immigrating individuals and states requirements, protocols, and restrictions to gain entrance to South Africa as a health care worker.

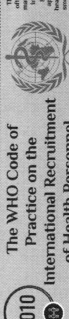

2010

The WHO Code of Practice on the International Recruitment of Health Personnel

The WHO Code of Practice on the International Recruitment of Health Personnel often referred to as "The Code" seeks to strengthen the understanding and ethical management of international health personnel recruitment through improved data, information, and international cooperation. The shortage of health personnel is a growing concern in many WHO Member States. The Code provides principles applicable to the international recruitment of health personnel to strengthen the health systems of developing countries, countries with economies in transition and small island states. The Code is an all-encompassing code of practice that validates the concerns of member states, and reaffirms the right to health for all.

Glennster, Roger and Kristina Shapplisk, A review of codes and protocols for the migration of health workers. September 2007. Accessed from: https://www.who.int/hrh/migration/compendium/2007_06_codesandprotocols.pdf?ua=1 and
Rudn, Jane, Robert J. Dolan, and Mark R. King, Standards for Cross-border Recruitment of Health Workers and their Implications for Policy Makers... and the National Science Foundation... Accessed from: https://www.who.int/hrh/migration... and
World Health Assembly. RESOLUTIONS AND DECISIONS WHA57.19 International migration of health personnel: a challenge for health systems in developing countries. May 2004. Accessed from: https://www.who.int/hrh/migration/background/en/ and
World Health Organization, WHO Global Code of Practice on the International Recruitment of Health Personnel, 2010.

Figure 6 (cont.)

provide an international basis for agreement on the mobility of workers, such as the General Agreement on Trades and Services, and regional labour mobility agreements, such as the South African Development Community Protocol. Codes and agreements explicitly related to health worker mobility increasingly converged to include similar goals in terms of eliminating exploitation in the recruitment process and upholding the right for workers to migrate, some also include support for universal health access. Considering that the inequitable distribution of healthcare workers is global and systemic, codes that reference the twin rights of workers and patients to secure the best conditions of work and care offer a productive contradiction echoing calls that "the conditions of work are the conditions of care" (Armstrong et al. 2020); and that the interests of patients and workers can and must be addressed in tandem (as discussed in Section 2).

Connell and Buchan (2011) explore the development of codes on the international recruitment of health workers, noting that the right to mobility is understood as a basic human right, and international migration is understood to offer important gains to society overall. However, the localized costs of health worker migration for sending regions often result in the need to develop policies to mitigate such costs and find a balance between a workers' right to move and the sustainability of health systems in sending regions. Connell and Buchan (2011) note the forerunners of the global code were focused on protecting workers from unethical recruiters, making sure they are supported at work and ensuring that disruption to health systems in sending countries is minimal.

Many of these codes are generalized in terms of agreed-upon recommendations, whereas stakeholders (unions, employers, migrants, governments) have very specific needs and interests that may contradict some or all aspects of recruitment addressed in voluntary codes. As these codes are voluntary, they include few enforcement or penalty options, and they are further constrained by poor health resource data, leading to uncertainty about the type of shortages occurring in different markets and the types of solutions that might be effective in addressing them. The WHO code and national precursors to it, while limited in application, have gone through a series of evolutions (Connell & Buchan 2011). Codes typically only apply to large public institutions or government health sectors, and as a result, potential migrants can escape regulation, making the codes often impossible to enforce (Connell & Buchan 2011; Mackey & Liang 2012). In addition to these limitations, the core moral dimension of such codes, that of ethical recruitment and fair labour agreements have been weakened over time. Early health worker brain drain discussions referenced compensation for the sending region, which was replaced by the idea of seeking "mutuality" through the process (Connell & Buchan 2011; Yeates and Pillinger 2019). This mutuality approach suggests other types of trade-offs be used to balance against source-region losses from health worker outmigration. This could include the use of health trade service agreements and training exchanges to compensate sending regions (Stilwell et al. 2004). In terms of their impact on sending countries, Connell and Buchan (2011) suggest the Code may have diverted rather than stemmed migration flows, and that improved working conditions in the source countries have proved more effective than codes in slowing outmigration.

Yeates and Pillinger (2019) provide an impressive analysis of international health worker migration and recruitment in terms of its emergence as a global social policy field. They note the substantial work undertaken by the ILO from the 1940s onward in terms of health worker migration through several conventions and recommendations focused on income security, employment agencies and service conventions, employment discrimination, the protection of migrant workers and social protection floor recommendations developed after 2012. Their detailed analysis of international organizations' policy development with reference to international health worker migration and recruitment notes the substantial work undertaken by the ILO, particularly with regard to the 1977 Nursing Personnel Recommendation, which Yeates and Pillinger (2019, p. 81) see as exceptional as the "first-ever multilateral agreement setting out the principles for international nurse recruitment and migration." This included guidelines on when countries should not recruit nurses internationally, but also what rights nurses should have in terms of the nature of employment and duties undertaken wherever employed. The ILO's role in this legislation has been cast as innovative, but ultimately underdeveloped in terms of monitoring and enforcement (Yeates & Pillinger 2019). However, the Nursing Personnel Recommendation did provide a basis for forms of global social governance that would emerge some 30 years later in health worker migration and recruitment. Yeates and Pillinger (2019, p 81) argue that the focus on the single occupation of nursing was widely supported and it "was a vital instrument in the elaboration of ILO's gender equality, labour migration and social protection regimes, WHO's right-to-health regime, and the UN's human rights and development regimes." The Nursing Personnel Recommendation was a non-binding instrument focused on one occupational group, which Yeates and Pillinger (2019) see as permitting the widespread support of the Recommendation, but note that despite its promises, it suffered from weak implementation. More recent analyses of the member state surveys for the ILO Nursing Personnel agreement have noted ongoing shortcomings in terms of policy coordination and rights monitoring for migrant nurses (Bourgeault et al. 2023).

Regarding subsequent global social policy development on this matter, Yeates and Pillinger (2019, p. 83) note that "WHO was a laggard in this nascent policy field" and suggest that this global social policy field evolved from liberal development approaches embracing health worker mobility through migration and educational harmonization, to more redistributive approaches supporting compensation and labour rights. Yeates and Pillinger (2019) argue that as these policy instruments have evolved culminating in the WHO Code, the redistributive and compensatory mechanisms have been less successfully embedded. In total, they express both the success and limitations of the development of the Code in terms of the multiple actors involved and state resistance to agree to anything surpassing minimal regulation. Overall, Yeates and Pillinger (2019) see the Code as "voluntary in nature, relies largely on self-regulation, and is devoid of an enforcement mechanism ... It is ill equipped to address global inequalities in health workforces that undermine achieving universal health care for all" (2019, p. 109). Despite the weaknesses of the Code, the final text managed to retain data sharing and implementation allowing a mechanism for monitoring the Code, with reports every three years, with the first reporting cycle in 2012 (Yeates & Pillinger 2019).

The WHO code is implicitly limited in its application considering the lack of data availability and the complexity surrounding health worker migration across an internationally uneven landscape. Only 44 per cent of countries considered to be in crisis based on their health work force density reported collecting relevant data on qualification and credential numbers. Only 23 per cent of all systems gathered data on workforce attrition, and fifty-seven resource-limited countries are identified as needing Human Resources Information Systems (Riley et al. 2012). More recent developments in support of the Global Strategy on Human Resources for Health: Workforce 2030 (adopted in May 2016), have attempted to address this data lacuna by encouraging Member States to engage in more robust data collection and information sharing through progressively implementing the NHWA which the WHO has created. National Health Workforce Accounts allow for the exchange of information about health worker migration among other health system factors, which also supports evaluation regarding the implementation of the Code. The WHO adopted the Global Strategy on Human Resources for Health: Workforce 2030 in May 2016 (WHO 2016a; Scheffler et al. 2018). The strategy includes milestones, one of which is that by 2020 member countries would make progress on developing a health workforce registry and by 2030 they will make progress towards self-sufficiency by halving their dependency on foreign-trained health professionals.

In terms of evaluation of the Code, in 2015 the WHO Director-General convened an Expert Advisory Group (EAG) to conduct the second review of the relevance and effectiveness of the Code. The EAG report confirmed the centrality of the Code to UHC and health security, and its increased recognition "as the universal ethical framework linking the international recruitment of health workers and the strengthening of health systems" (WHO 2020b, p. 2). The report argued the full implementation of the Code was needed to achieve UHC and noted the synergies of the Code with other global agendas, including Global Agenda on the Nursing and Midwifery workforce. The EAG found significant gaps in the Code's implementation that deemed it insufficient to realize the Code's full potential to meet the SDGs and UHC. Table 4 outlines the gaps identified by the EAG in more detail.

The EAG also noted that health workforce density and UHC service coverage index should be used to identify countries with the most pressing UHC workforce challenges. In response to this, a new safeguards and support list was developed that listed forty-seven countries facing the most pressing workforce challenges linked to achieving UHC. Countries on this list were identified as being prioritized for health system–related supports and provided with safeguards to discourage international recruitment of health personnel (WHO 2021c). Figure 7 illustrates the countries on the safeguard list and the density of health workers (all of which are below the SDG threshold of 44.5 per 10,000 population).

Clemens and Dempster (2021) explore the safeguard list and make the argument that rather than banning international recruitment, the safeguard list allows for recruitment, if it meets the mutually beneficial criteria of the Code. They go on to suggest how countries can design sustainable and ethical migration agreements through examples such as Global Skill Partnerships and Investment in health systems. Recalling Section 3, the reality of existing healthcare worker shortages in countries on the safeguard list means they are already engaged in agreements that promote the mobility of healthcare workers in terms of training and exchange. This suggests there are possibilities for more mutually beneficial approaches to health worker mobility to be further developed.

In charting the evolution of codes related to the international migration and recruitment of healthcare workers, it is worth noting the convergence of international agreements and instruments relevant to this issue, which was an issue the EAG noted in detail. The WHO Code and its implementation is supported through other WHO agendas such as the Global Strategy on HRH 2030, UHC and the SDGs. In addition, the recently agreed upon Global Compact on Safe, Regular and Orderly Migration (GCM) is the first globally negotiated cooperative framework that commits to the principle of "gender-responsive" policy responses to migration (UNGA 2018), a feature that is highly relevant to the

Table 4 Gaps identified by the Expert Advisory Group report on the WHO Code (WHO 2020b)

Gaps	Why	EAG Recommendations to Fix Gaps in the WHO Code	Examples of Ways to Close Gaps
Need to strengthen the technical cooperation with Member States, the capacity of the WHO Secretariat and engagement with relevant non-State actors (22)	• Will ensure the Code's relevance and full application (20) • Can further drive Code implementation and effectiveness and ensure the accountability of governments Closing this gap allows the acceleration of implementation of the Code	Develop Global Guidance and Tools: Code User and Implementation Guide, Repository and Best Practices on Bilateral Agreements, Global Data Report on International Health Worker Mobility, Estimation of education costs and remittances and Approaches to better understand and improve the lived experience of migrant health workers Strengthen engagement with private sector actors, including complementary hospital, trade union and recruiter codes. (22)	• Raise awareness and Code engagement among health workers, public and private employers, regulatory bodies, public and private sector recruitment agencies, academia and civil society (20) • Strengthen the synergies and coherence between the Code, and other actors: that is, employers, health workers and recruiters (20)

Ability for WHO Member States to mobilize investments in education, recruitment and retention of health workers (22) Emphasizing the central importance of health workforce education and employment to the UHC agenda (23)	• Will provide support for a global public good • to effectively deliver UHC • Allows safeguards and support for healthcare workers	Commit multi-year flexible funds towards Code implementation (22) Director-General to allocate sufficient nonearmarked funds to support the Secretariat's health workforce activities. (23)	• Invest in developing countries and economies in transition to retain the health workers they need (12) • Creation of global partnerships to invest in skills development in countries of origin to better meet global labour demand (10) Nursing was the example given during deliberations, with investment in nursing education in countries of origin to help meet nursing shortages in others (10)

Note: Gaps in the WHO code reported by the EAG (Expert Advisory Group).

Source: *Director*-General, Report of the WHO Expert Advisory Group on the Relevance and Effectiveness of the WHO Global Code of Practice on the International Recruitment of Health Personnel. *May 2020.* http4:ilVapps.wtio.intlgbi cbwha.pdf_filca/WHA73/^A73_9-en.pdf

The EAG recommends a further assessment of the Code's relevance and effectiveness to be considered following the fifth round of national reporting in 2023–2024 and to be presented to the 79th WHA (23).

WHO health workforce support and safeguards list 2023

The threshold for the universal health coverage service coverage index for the WHO health workforce support and safeguards list 2023 has been increased from 50 (the value used for the 2020 list) to 55.

Source: WHO · Created with Datawrapper

Figure 7 Safeguard and support list countries and density of health workers (Source WHO NHWA portal)

mobility of health workers considering the gendered features of the healthcare workforce. The EAG remarked on these convergences, noting the SDGs have resulted in the need for a more coherent approach to securing a better future for all, especially regarding building sustainable health workforces and strengthening health systems everywhere. The UHC agenda also requires Member States to support rather than compromise the abilities of all states to reach such goals. The EAG also noted the Code is highly relevant to the Global compact and the UN Network on Migration, where issues of health worker mobility are discussed (WHO 2020b). Figure 8 illustrates the convergence of these international agreements.

4.3 Promising Policy Responses to Health Worker Mobility

Promising policy responses to the mobility of healthcare workers, including those that allow for mutuality in terms of the benefits accrued to sending and receiving countries, are increasingly evident. They include examples that operate at different scales, from the WHO Code itself, to regional agreements that promote labour mobility and the protection of migrants, to the creative use of bilateral labour agreements and skills mobility agreements that protect mutually beneficial or triple win outcomes for sending and receiving countries and migrants themselves. Solutions also include national approaches to the effective incorporation of internationally educated healthcare workers into national

Figure 8 Convergence of international agreements related to the international recruitment and migration of healthcare workers (graphic by Samantha Zani)

health systems using bridging programs and occupational ombudsmen to monitor the fair incorporation of foreign-trained professionals.

4.3.1 Regional Agreements

A growing number of regional agreements promote the migration of healthcare
workers either explicitly, or as part of a wider labour mobility agreements. The
EU is one of the leading cases, offering "the best example we have of the
application of the principles of market liberalization to real live health services
by supranational bodies" (Jarman & Greer 2010, p. 158). European integration
provides a valuable case for understanding how increased regionalization
influences the migration of high-skilled workers. Enhanced employment and
educational options are central to EU regional development plans, driven by an
emphasis on the harmonization of training and credential assessment. The
Bologna Process established the framework for the EHEA, which was officially
launched in March 2010 (Reinalda 2008). Creating the EHEA depended on
a "tuning" process for the alignment of education systems and competencies
across the region (Walton-Roberts 2014). Directive 2005/36/EC of the
European Parliament on the recognition of professional qualifications "consoli-
dated a system of mutual recognition . . . [that] provides for automatic recognition for a limited number of professions based on harmonised minimum training
requirements (sectoral professions), a general system for the recognition of
evidence of training and automatic recognition of professional experience.
Directive 2005/36/EC also established a new system of free provision of
services."[10]

Under Directive 2005/36/EC, automatic recognition applies to seven "sectoral" professions: medical doctor, general care nurse, dentist, midwife, veter-
inary surgeon, pharmacist and architect based on coordination of minimum
training conditions. The resultant EU Directive 2005/36/EC also applies in the
EEA area (Norway, Iceland, Liechtenstein) and the Swiss Confederation.
Fourteen countries employed the resultant assessment of competencies matrix,
which compares qualifications across EU member states (Cowan & Wilson-
Barnett 2006). The result has been a comprehensive continual effort at educational and training alignment to create minimum agreed-upon competencies
that allow for, and encourage, professional mobility throughout the EU. This
model of "tuning" candidates' training and competencies across national bor-
ders offers an example of how to support and effectively implement MRAs that
promote quality training to support free and fair labour mobility.

---

[10] https://eur-lex.europa.eu/legal-content/EN/TXT/?uri=celex:32005L0036.

ASEAN member countries Brunei, Cambodia, Indonesia, Laos, Malaysia, Myanmar, Philippines, Singapore, Thailand and Vietnam are party to the ASEAN Framework Agreement on Services (AFAS) to liberalize trade and services agreements beyond those undertaken through GATS. The path for trade in services liberalization was discussed in the ASEAN vision 2020 partnership in Dynamic Development (approved June 17, 1997), which charts a path toward the creation of an ASEAN Economic Region. ASEAN mode 4 commitments in the AFAS process are modest. ASEAN has, however, made significant strides through the adoption of MRAs to facilitate the free mobility of skilled workers within the ASEAN region. While ASEAN member states' progress toward deepening regional integration efforts are incomplete, professional MRAs are one of the few areas where the Economic Community blueprint is adding value (Gootiiz & Mattoo 2017). Eight professions are included in MRAs, medical doctor, dentist, surveyor, architect, accounting, engineer, nurse and tourism professional (Fukunaga 2015). The first seven professions are regulated and, in a process like that undertaken in the Bologna process, require a training framework be developed to allow for comparison and agreement on minimum training standards (Aungsuroch & Gunawan 2015). Unlike the EU however, ASEAN MRAs are only for select professions, and general labour mobility is not allowed throughout the ASEAN region. MRAs may therefore still be hampered by immigration regulations imposed by ASEAN member states (Fukunaga 2015). One assessment of the ASEAN MRA framework is that rather than promote the mobility of professionals between ASEAN Member States, it will begin by enhancing the quality of local professional training across the region (Fukunaga 2015). While the current effectiveness of the MRA in the ASEAN has been slow to demonstrate success, the aims of the MRA extend beyond trade in services and offers the promise of improved training across the region through commitments to deeper integration in nurse education and professional development, as well as professional mobility. As nursing scholars in Indonesian recognize: "AEC as a gate for nurse mobility is expected to be a good deal to reduce jobless in Indonesia, increase the quality of Indonesian nurses by providing training, develop nursing curricula, and improve the language proficiency and competency of nurses." (Aungsuroch & Gunawan 2015, p. 1579).

Other treaties include the Trans-Tasman Mutual Recognition Act 1997, which includes mobility between New Zealand (NZ) and Australia, and the Caricom Treaty of Chaguramas, which established the Caribbean Community and Common Market or CARICOM. Signed by Barbados, Guyana, Jamaica, and Trinidad and Tobago, it created the Caribbean Single Market and Economy which promotes free movement of labour.

4.3.2 Bilateral Agreements

There have been calls for international health worker migration to be shaped by "triple win" or fair migration policies that provide benefits for sending and receiving countries, as well as for migrant workers themselves. The WHO Code provides a global framework for countries to use as a guide when entering into bilateral or regional agreements for health worker mobility to promote cooperation and coordination (Dhillon et al. 2010). However, lower-income nations often face the challenge of bilateral agreements failing to address the negative effects associated with the outmigration of health workers, as lower-income nations often have less capacity and political capital to demand such provisions in bilateral agreements.

The Philippines has invested heavily in promoting overseas employment opportunities for its citizens, and since the 1970s labour out-migration has become a national strategy for improving national economic growth (Sikorski 1994). The Philippines has one of the most robust systems for supporting nurse migration and leads international supply, exporting nurses to over fifty nations (Ortiga 2018b). Nurse education is heavily privatized in the Philippines, as is the facilitation of nurse migration. Private interests have a great deal of power over migrants and the migration process itself (Masselink & Lee 2010). Nursing schools in the Philippines are seen as "migrant institutions," and there are direct pipelines between nursing schools in the Philippines and American or UK hospitals (Ortiga 2018b). Several Canadian provinces have secured bilateral agreements, or MOUs with the Philippines in the past, including Alberta, Manitoba, British Colombia and Saskatchewan (Blank 2011). Although the MOUs do not directly govern nurses' status in Canada, they outline a pathway to permanent settlement. Moreover, they all focus on promoting collaboration between the respective provinces and the Philippine government, in addition to promoting development in the sending nation through various compensatory or mutuality agreements and, as such, have been noted as best practices by the Filipino government (Blank 2011). The Philippines is an important actor in the search for mutually beneficial approaches to nurse mobility, and their report to National Reporting Instrument Reports Database (2018) on the implementation of the WHO Code specifically identified the need for more assistance in negotiating and dealing with receiving nations in order to better safeguard worker rights and improve nurse migration outcomes.

The Indian state, in comparison with the Philippines, presents itself as a facilitator, not promoter of labour migration (Walton-Roberts 2015a). The increase in international migration of nurses from India has coincided with a rapid increase in private nursing educational institutions in India; however, the expansion is not driven only by migrant demand (Oda et al. 2018). The Government of India also contributes to migration drivers by signing labour migration MOUs with countries that already have long-running migration flows from India (Wickramasekara 2012; Sasikumar & Thimothy 2015). The Government of India's approach to nurse migration focuses on the regulation of commercial interests (Timmons et al. 2016; Varghese 2020), together with state control over migration to specific geographical markets (Walton-Roberts et al. 2022). Although the Indian state has sought to address recruiter exploitation of nurses, its adoption of "protective" policies has overwhelmingly positioned women's mobility as the problem, rather than the structures that exploit them (Walton-Roberts & Rajan 2020). While there is evidence of the increased use of bilateral agreements being reported by WHO member states in their reporting to the WHO Code (WHO 2017a) there are immense differences regarding what bilateral agreements state in theory, and what happens in practice. For example, India has a range of MOUs signed with other countries that relate to "manpower" or have specific health worker references regarding training and professional exchanges. When examined in more detail, however, some of these agreements offer relatively little detail about the rights of workers and the conditions of labour mobility beyond vague references to partnerships. This is evident in the case of India's relationship with the UAE, where even though there is a sizeable flow of health workers (nurses and doctors) occurring between India and UAE, there is no specific mention of nurses in MOUs between the two countries regarding "manpower" agreements (Walton-Roberts & Khadria 2023).

4.3.3 National Agreements

There are also a series of promising national approaches to the integration of internationally trained health workers. Ivy Bourgeault et al. (2022), explore the importance of bridging programs for professional migration and integration, an area that has not been deeply researched. In their conceptual model of integration frameworks, bridging programs reside at the meso level. Bridging programs focus on individual needs but also systemic ones in terms of changing the outlook and orientation of higher education institutions to understand the needs of different populations who enter the health workforce. This is highly important to the process of transferring the value embodied in internationally trained workers to new national health system contexts. Bourgeault et al. (2022) note how clinical placements are a challenge to secure for many migrant health workers, but they are vital to the success of bridging programs. Flexible program design and public institutions partnerships are also key, as are links to professional associations and employers. While such coordination between stakeholders is challenging, the consequences of COVID-19 have encouraged governments to become active in encouraging and facilitating more flexible and responsive integration processes for internationally trained healthcare workers.[11]

Baumann et al. (2022) further explore the issue of matching internationally trained health professionals into Canadian health labour markets, noting the detachment between immigration policy and labour market planning. They focus on a project developed to match internationally trained nurses to full-time employment with various employers. Their project established that best practices include a mandate and vision that engages in targeted recruitment and recognizes the community they are serving, creating well-developed integration programs and dedicated employer committees that focus on diversity.

Other important regulatory responses at the national level in destination countries are ombudsmen and fairness commissions. These regulate fair access to professions for internationally educated health professionals and encourage innovations in workplace integration and credential and professional competency assessment. In Ontario, Canada, two thirds of regulated trades are health related. Public safety, as well as fairness in access for internationally trained professionals, needs to be balanced in these contexts. In 2006, the "Fair Access to Regulated Professions" Act was passed, including the creation of the Ontario Fairness Commissioner (OFC) (Türegün 2017). The OFC oversees the work of 42 regulatory bodies and 22 trades in Ontario and is mandated to hold professional regulatory bodies to account for how they process international applicants. The OFC stipulates that testing should be fair, transparent and objective, and that fees charged to applicants should be only cost recovery (Jafri 2022). In many cases, the work of the OFC has resulted in novel approaches to improve the credential assessment process. Other provinces have also addressed the issue of international applicants seeking to enter regulated professions with a Fairness commissioner, including Nova Scotia (2008) and Manitoba (2009) (Jafri 2022). In Quebec, a similar ombudsman role expanded in 2009. Nonetheless, there is still much work to do in this area. For example, the 2018–2019 OFC annual report (Government of Ontario 2019) indicated that although improvements have been made over time, 40 per cent of the professional regulatory bodies were still not meeting their legislated requirements. State policy intervention that can continuously improve the processes that govern the integration of internationally trained health workers remains a key policy issue.

---

[11] See www.hhr-rhs.ca/en/tools/covid-19/innovations-db.html for a database of Health Workforce Strategies in Response to the COVID-19 Pandemic.

Other national responses to the international migration of health professionals include Australia's response, which is to move to "peak" national-level regulators where the process of application and assessment is streamlined. Requirements for licensure include an educational standard, experience or an apprenticeship/practicum, an examination, an ethical or moral hurdle, and citizenship/residency. And in some cases, and especially relevant for immigrants, is a minimum language fluency. Some groups might regulate more than one function (certification and regulation), but little research has examined whether overlapping functions within such institutions is a good idea. Many self-regulating groups also work in the public sector, which means they do not face competition in the normal sense, with the state often the sole funder and seller of services, and the role of intermediaries (schools, hospital boards) in the process can make assessment and regulation even more complicated (Sweetman 2022).

4.4 Conclusion

The WHO Global Code represents the culmination of previous codes that have been developed, in that it tries to achieve a balance between the interests of healthcare workers and source countries and promote practices that allow health worker migration to have a positive impact on health systems overall. The growing importance of the provision of adequate health care to all societies is an indicator of global social policy demands and expectations that accompany ongoing societal development (as discussed in Section 3 regarding the build back better agenda). The evolution of various codes to monitor the global circulation and mobility of health workers has matured in the sense that there is now a clear convergence of international instruments and tools to promote both the rights and protections of migrant health workers, but also to work to protect health systems globally. The development of the 2030 strategy for human health resources, the creation of the NHWA information sharing portal, and the WHO International Platform on Health Worker Mobility, signal efforts to develop better health workforce data systems at all scales. Combined with the global context of the SDGs, the commitment to UHC and the Global Compact on Migration, reveal an invigorated landscape for more collaborative approaches to ameliorating the potential damage unchecked international health worker recruitment and migration might cause. While there are promising practices emerging, the WHO Code has been critiqued as not being fit for the purpose it is designed, mainly because it is unenforceable (Yeates & Pillinger 2019), and not all stakeholders are fully aware of its relevance to health worker mobility (Bourgeault et al. 2016). Despite these shortcomings, other promising practices continue to emerge, including the inclusion of international health worker mobility in regional agreements that promote mutual recognition of credentials, or form frameworks for regional learning exchanges in health professional training. Bilateral agreements continue to emerge that include health worker mobility, such as those developed with the Philippines, as well as using WHO Code feedback opportunities to highlight the need for greater technical assistance to design and better implement bilateral agreements in support of mutuality as outlined in the WHO Code.

At the national scale, receiving countries are also developing innovative policies to improve the inclusion of internationally trained health workers into domestic labour markets. Approaches, such as bridging programs, and ombudsmen and fairness commissioners, suggest that leading receiving countries recognize their moral responsibility to maximize the opportunities for the inclusion of international health workers. Deeper system change, however, is still needed, including better data collection, and sharing to understand the dynamics of health worker migration, and the degree to which all countries are achieving sustainability in their health workforce through improved training and retention.

5 Conclusion

The global migration of healthcare workers is a significant focus of an emerging global social policy field (Yeates and Pillinger 2019). As discussed in section one the global circulation of healthcare workers has a history marked by colonial remnants and the ongoing influence of colonial networks. The colonial context informs the type of health systems that emerged, as well as the geography of migration flows and the processes that shape it, including the racial and cultural hierarchies that migrant workers are stratified into. The globalized tendencies embedded in health worker migration unsettle notions of stand-alone *national* healthcare systems. Rather, what we see is the formation of health professional training and provisioning systems that emerged under the colonial yoke of uneven development and have continued under increasingly globally connected yet unequal systems where health worker distribution at all scales (local, regional, international) has immense consequences. These processes are also deeply gendered, reflecting the devaluation of care and social reproduction globally.

Section 1 outlined the evolution of health worker migration from ex-colonies to core economies as healthcare systems expanded in the post-WWII period, especially illustrated by the growth of the NHS in the UK and the sourcing and inclusion of health workers from the Caribbean and Indian sub-continent. In Europe and North America in the 1960s, economic growth and the inclusion of women in non-traditional labour market activities created a demand for nurses, which was secured through reliance on sending countries in Asia, particularly the Philippines. Healthcare worker migration circuits were also developing within regional linguistic grouping, such as Lusophone and Francophone networks, and these continue to transform particularly through the development of regional and bilateral agreements. By the 1970s, the economic growth in the Petro states of the Middle East also created new circuits for healthcare worker recruitment, and these corridors have become part of wider Anglophone migratory circuits that serve both domestic populations, as well growing regional medical tourism hubs.

The significance of health worker mobility for the development of effective health systems everywhere and for everyone has been a global concern since the 1960s. However, by the 1990s the situation of health worker migration and its consequences on vulnerable health systems became acute, reaching a zenith when South Africa faced the joint and compounding challenges of the AIDS epidemic and intense "poaching" of their health workers by core countries. This situation was reflective of broader uneven economic development, and the lack of investment in healthcare systems, particularly in low- and middle-income nations where SAPs had demanded public investment be curtailed in order to meet fiscal restraint. International organizations such as the ILO and WHO continue to highlight this social policy field, but with the arrival of the COVID-19 pandemic, the matter has become more acute for all levels of government.

The geography of health worker migration has become more complex in the past few years, and while the dominant pattern of movement from Global South to North remains in place, we have seen other patterns emerge (South-South and East-West), as well as new forms of mobility marked by different temporal process (temporary, circular and migration for career development and training). These migration patterns are indicative of a highly dynamic global circulatory system for healthcare workers, which challenges the notion of health systems being nationally bounded and directed. Layered onto this complexity is the reality of the heterogeneous nature of healthcare systems, including state and non-state, and private and publicly funded systems, and the emergence of regional medical hubs in Asia and the Middle East serving increased medical tourism demands.

To further assess the ethical and political grounding of health worker mobility, Section 2 outlined a perspective informed by feminist political economy that centred on issue of care. The consequences of the COVID-19 pandemic have concentrated the attention of governments and the public on health systems, essential workers and the reality of care needs and those who provide it and how it is resourced and protected. Care is vital for human well-being but has been devalued in part because of its conflation with essentialized feminine traits, and its commodification and marketization under processes of neoliberal governance. This has intensified norms that suggest the market, rather than the state, is expected to provide care services. This marketization of care permits the intersection of corporate capital interests with societal traditions and norms of devaluing and making invisible the work of women, especially racialized women and other marginalized groups. Theories of care, including the care diamond, which permits an understanding of the welfare mix in place in different national systems, include how care is distributed across the market, the state, the family and the self. These nationally determined care diamonds can be connected through transnational or global care chains, that connect distinct places through chains of care workers whose migration substitutes for the care that would be provided, either by other citizens or by state welfare systems. In moving to provide this care elsewhere, migrants (typically racialized women from low- and middle-income nations) withdraw their own care labour from their families, leaving someone else to substitute care in their place, and/or provide cash in the form of remittances to support their families' sustenance.

Our consideration of how care is provided must also be informed by the ethics of care. The basic fact that at some points in our lives all humans need care clearly communicates the universal and essential nature of this relationship. Issues of human dignity, vulnerability and quality of life have inspired critical approaches to the assessment of who provides care for whom and under what conditions. Such approaches include work on vulnerability and the human condition (Fineman 2008), which posits that the very universal nature of care places the state in the position of being responsible for and responsive to this reality.

The international recruitment of healthcare workers is the focus of several international agreements focused on health, development and migrant rights. This includes the commitment to advance UHC through investment in health systems, which requires the right numbers, distribution and skill mix of healthcare workers. Health worker migration is also central to most of the SDGs, including those focused on migration, education, gender and health care. This reality does appear to be making some headway in the wake of the COVID-19 pandemic. National responses to the consequences of COVID-19 have opened a portal, acknowledging the need to invest in health and care infrastructure, including healthcare workforces, building resilient health systems and recognizing the centrality and essential nature of care for the young, the old and differently abled. Under the theme of "building back better" several examples of such responses are laid out in Section 2, revealing both the magnitude and geographical comprehensiveness of such proposals and initiatives, but also their fragility considering constantly changing agendas.

Section 3 focuses more specifically on factors of migration and examines the vital role of health workers in the sustainability and quality of health services. It also considered how the COVID-19 pandemic has tested and stressed health workers and systems. As systems have buckled under pandemic strains, the recruitment of internationally trained health workers is again a leading health workforce option states are pursuing. Section 3 considers the basic conceptual formulations of labour migration, paying attention to migration drivers, including predisposing, proximate, precipitating and mediating drivers, and their specific relevance to cases involving health workers. Conceptualizing how migrant labour is included in receiving country's labour markets is also explored, revealing again the significance of gender, race and other intersectional variables in terms of migrant worker inclusion, exploitation and stratification. The role of migrant intermediaries in the growing market for health workers is further detailed in terms of labour market experiences. Intermediaries play an important role because many health occupations are regulated, demanding effective labour market information, since both visa and workplace demands increase the value and importance of the information and guidance intermediaries can provide. The relevance and importance of intermediaries for health worker migrants have made them a key focus of health worker migration codes through ethical migration demands that protect migrant workers from exploitation and fraud while improving workplace integration.

Complementing analysis of the experiences of migrant health workers in receiving countries is that of understanding what their departure means for sending nations. Here results from a four-country study looking at source country perspectives on health worker migration are discussed to reveal the diversity of experiences across different national contexts (India, Philippines, Jamaica and South Africa), but also to reveal some of the universal concerns in terms of the lack of engagement with global instruments such as the WHO Code, and the general absence of collaboration between health and migration ministries within sending country governments. These types of comparative studies allow us to recognize how health worker outmigration can distort source country training systems, perpetuating the outflow of health workers to service global, rather than national healthcare needs. In some cases, though, there is evidence of sending countries engaging with the international market, as well as strategizing on how to attract workers to return back to their homes and improving worker retention. This area of policy remains a promising, but underutilized solution to excess outmigration.

Adding to the diversity of healthcare worker migration routes is the increasing use of transit country migration, and here we can appreciate the value of connecting the care diamond and chain concept to understand how state's migration systems frame mobility options. Policies that limit permanent residence for migrant workers will frame decisions about settlement and subsequent pathways. Broader policy options regarding onward migration and mobility also frame transit migration option values that can be planned over the long term through multiple migration steps (Artuc & Ozden 2018). In effect this means that regional formation membership changes, such as Brexit, have important effects for other geographic regions. In the case of Brexit health worker migrant decision-making will be framed by the options presented or removed with the UK's departure from the EU.

A further development considered in Section 3 is the distinction of foreign-trained to foreign-born workers, and here we can see the potential influence of the evolving globalization of health training. Continuous health professional development imposes increasingly complex demands on national training systems, and this is particularly challenging for low- and middle-income nations, including small states (islands and otherwise), that have limited capacity to provide upgraded training. Using data from the NHWA Portal provides an interesting if partial insight into this phenomenon. It reveals cases of intra-regional mobility in the training of health workers (EU member states), small island states where training capacity is constrained, low-income nations that depend on official aid partnerships for health training (including the growing presence of China and long-term role of Cuba in this regard), as well as Gulf nations where domestic health labour markets and training systems are nascent.

Section 4 examines policy responses to health worker mobilities paying particular attention to global analysis of this emergent policy field, and the international response in terms of the evolution of voluntary codes on the international recruitment of health personnel. These voluntary codes have evolved to provide relatively limited commitments on the part of Member States to promote the ethical recruitment of healthcare workers while protecting the capacity of health systems globally. Voluntary codes are exactly that, voluntary, and are therefore underpowered in terms of penalties and enforcement options, but they do provide an increasingly common lexicon for Member States to understand the consequence of their actions in terms of health worker migration and encourage collaboration on health worker international recruitment. The maturity of the WHO Code is also evident as more reporting rounds are completed, and the code dovetails with other landmark international agreements on issues such as UHC, SDGs and the Global Compact on Migration. Recent expert advisory group reports on the WHO Code have noted the gaps evident while upholding the significance of the WHO Code and its relevance to these other global agreements. Important gaps identified in the review of the WHO Code include the need for enhanced technical cooperation across stakeholders, increase investment in health training, and the importance of health worker training for the UHC agenda. The ongoing revisions to the list of countries on the safeguard and support list (those not currently and not projected to not meet the SDG threshold for health worker density), is a timely update that will focus the attention of all nations to protect the most vulnerable, as well as develop innovative cooperation agreements that uphold the ideals of mutuality when states develop health worker mobility agreements.

Section 4 also reviews promising policy responses in terms of regional and bilateral agreements, and national policies that promote the full and effective integration of internationally trained health professionals. Understanding health worker international recruitment and migration demands we employ a global lens. The issue has surpassed being a concern for individual nation states, it is no longer about how individual states manage specific health worker shortages to their own agendas. The training and mobility of health workers is an issue framed by the interests of all states, which all have a responsibility to develop sustainable health workforce policies that reduce reliance on migrant workers while increasing international technical supports and partnerships that enhance states' ability to achieve UHC. Meeting many of the international goals we have set for ourselves in the SDGs demands international collaboration and agreement. The framework is in place, and the commitment to support its development has been momentarily enhanced through the consequences of the COVID-19 pandemic. Vigilance in continual assessment of outcomes and practices of all states demands much greater stakeholder collaboration nationally, regionally and globally. Technical support and improved data collection and sharing are allowing us to understand how the international mobility of health workers for training, education and work unsettle our assumptions about the nationally bounded nature of healthcare systems.

Abbreviations

AFAS	ASEAN Framework Agreement on Services
ASEAN	Association of Southeast Asian Nations
B3 W	Build Back Better World Partnership
CARICOM	The Caribbean Community and Common Market
COVID-19	coronavirus disease
EAG	Expert Advisory Group
EHEA	European Higher Education Area
EIB	European Investment Bank
EU	European Union
GATS	General Agreement on Trade in Services
GCC	Gulf Co-operation Council
GCM	Global Compact on Safe, Regular and Orderly Migration
ICN	International Council of Nurses
IENs	Internationally Educated Nurses
ILO	International Labour Organization
MD	Medical Doctor
MOUs	Memoranda of Understanding
MRA	Mutual Recognition Agreement
MW	Midwifery Personnel
N	Nursing Personnel
NHS	National Health Service
NHWA	National Health Workforce Accounts
NZ	New Zealand
OECD	Organisation for Economic Co-operation and Development
OFC	Ontario Fairness Commissioner
SADC	Southern Africa Development Community
SAPs	Structural Adjustment Programs
SDGs	sustainable development goals
SEA	South-East Asian
UAE	United Arab Emirates
UHC	Universal Health Coverage
UK	United Kingdom
UN	United Nations
UNESCO	United Nations Educational, Scientific and Cultural Organisation
USA	United States of America
WHA	World Health Assembly
WHO	World Health Organisation

References

Abdel-Razeq, H., Barbar, M., Shamieh, O. & Mansour, A. (2020). Oncology medical training and practice: Managing Jordan's brain drain through brain train-The King Hussein cancer center experience. *JCO Global Oncology*, 6, 1041–1045. https://doi.org/10.1200/GO.20.00141.

Adepoju, A. (2001). Regional organizations and intra-regional migration in Sub-Saharan Africa: Challenges and prospects. *International Migration*, 39(6), 43–60.

Adhikari, R. (2019). *Migrant health professionals and the global labour market: The dreams and traps of Nepali nurses*. New York: Routledge.

Alameddine, M., Kharroubi, S. A., Dumit, N. Y. et al. (2019). What made Lebanese emigrant nurses leave and what would bring them back? A cross-sectional survey. *International Journal of Nursing Studies*, 103, 103497.

Al-Hanawi, M. K., Khan, S. A. & Al-Borie, H. M. (2019). Healthcare human resource development in Saudi Arabia: Emerging challenges and opportunities – a critical review. *Public Health Reviews*, 40(1), 1–16.

Al-Harahsheh, S., White, D., Ali, A. F. et al. (2020). Nursing and midwifery workforce development. *World Innovation Summit for Health and Qatar Foundation, Policy Briefing*. September 15.

Al-Jarallah, K., Moussa, M. & Al-Khanfar, K. F. (2010). The physician workforce in Kuwait to the year 2020. *The International Journal of Health Planning and Management*, 25(1), 49–62. https://doi.org/10.1002/hpm.983.

Alluhidan, M., Tashkandi, N., Alblowi, F. et al. (2020). Challenges and policy opportunities in nursing in Saudi Arabia. *Human Resources for Health*, 18(98), 1–10. https://doi.org/10.1186/s12960-020-00535-2.

Amrith, M. (2017). *Caring for strangers: Filipino medical workers in Asia*. Copenhagen: NIAS Press.

Armstrong, P., Armstrong, H., Choiniere, J., Lowndes, R. & Struthers, J. (2020). *Re-imagining long-term residential care in the COVID-19 crisis*. Ottawa: Canadian Centre for Policy Alternatives.

Arnold, D. (1993). *Colonizing the body: State medicine and epidemic disease in nineteenth-century India*. Berkeley, CA: University of California Press.

Artuc, E. & Ozden, C. (2018). Transit migration: All roads lead to America. *The Economic Journal*, 128(612), F306–F334.

Asia-Pacific SDG Partnership. (2021). *Responding to the COVID-19 pandemic: Leaving no country behind*. Bangkok: United Nations, Asian Development Bank, and United Nations Development Programme.

Aungsuroch, Y. & Gunawan, J. (2015). Nurse preparation towards ASEAN economic community 2015. *International Journal of Health Science and Research*, 5(3), 365–372.

Awases, M., Gbary, A., Nyoni, J. & Chatora, R. (2003). *Migration of health professionals in six countries: A synthesis report*. Brazzaville: World Health Organisation Regional Office for Africa, pp. 1–77.

Bakan, A. B. & Stasiulis, D. (Eds.). (1997). *Not one of the family: Foreign domestic workers in Canada*. Toronto: University of Toronto Press.

Bala, P. (Ed.). (2012). *Contesting colonial authority: Medicine and indigenous responses in nineteenth-and twentieth-century India*. Lanham, MD: Lexington Books.

Bandyopadhyny, S., Thomas, H. S., Gurung, B. et al. (2020). Global health education in medical schools (GHEMS): A national, collaborative study of medical curricula. *BMC Medical Education*, 20(389), 1–17.

Barocas, J., Gounder, C. & Madad, S. (2021). Just-in-time versus just-in-case pandemic preparedness. *Health Affairs Forefront*. February 12.

Baumann, A. & Blythe, J. (2008). Globalization of higher education in nursing. *OJIN: The Online Journal of Issues in Nursing*, 13(2), 1–10.

Baumann, A., Crea-Arsenio, M. & Antonipillai, V. (2022). Global migration and key issues in workforce integration of skilled health workers. In M. Walton-Roberts, ed., *Global migration, gender, and health professional credentials*. Toronto: University of Toronto Press, pp. 95–109.

Betelhem, J., Pek, E., Olah, A. & Banfai, B. (2017). Current characteristics of the Hungarian nurses' workforce. In M. Pajnkihar, D. Vrbnjak & G. Stiglic, eds., *Teaching and learning in nursing*. Croatia: InTech, pp. 99–122. https://doi.org/10.5772/67427.

Blank, N. R. (2011). Making migration policy: Reflections on the Philippines' bilateral labor agreements. *Asian Politics & Policy*, 3(2), 185–205. https://doi.org/10.1111/j.1943-0787.2011.01255.x.

Bleakley, A., Brice, J. & Bligh, J. (2008). Thinking the post-colonial in medical education. *Medical Education*, 42(3), 266–270.

Boros, L., Dudás, G., Ilcsikné Makra, Z., Morar, C. & Pál, V. (2022). The migration of health care professionals from Hungary: Global flows and local responses. *Deturope*, 14(1), 164–188.

Boucher, A. (2007). Skill, migration and gender in Australia and Canada: The case of gender-based analysis. *Australian Journal of Political Science*, 42(3), 383–401.

Bourgeault, I., Atanackovic, J. & Neiterman, E. (2022). Gendering integration pathways: Migrating health professionals to Canada. In M. Walton-Roberts, ed., *Global migration, gender, and health professional credentials*. Toronto: University of Toronto Press, pp. 109–125.

Bourgeault, I. L., Labonté, R., Packer, C., Runnels, V. & Tomblin-Murphy, G. (2016). Knowledge and potential impact of the WHO global code of practice on the international recruitment of health personnel: Does it matter for source and destination country stakeholders? *Human Resources for Health*, 14(1), 121–123.

Bourgeault, I. L., Runnels, V., Atanackovic, J., Spitzer, D. & Walton-Roberts, M. (2021). Hiding in plain sight: The absence of consideration of the gendered dimensions in "source" country perspectives on health worker migration. *Human Resources for Health*, 19(1), 1–13.

Bourgeault, I. L., Spitzer, D. & Walton-Roberts, M. (2023). Complexities of health and care worker migration pathways and corresponding international reporting requirements. *Human Resources for Health*, 21(1), 1–9.

Britnell, M. (2019). *Human: Solving the global workforce crisis in healthcare*. Oxford: Oxford University Press.

Brookes, G. & Nuku, K. K. (2020). Why we aren't celebrating Florence's birthday. *Kai Tiaki Nursing New Zealand*, 26(3), 34–35.

Brown, R. P. C. & Connell, J. (2004). The migration of doctors and nurses from South Pacific Island Nations. *Social Science and Medicine*, 58(11), 2193–2210. https://doi.org/10.1016/j.socscimed.2003.08.020.

Brush, B. L. & Sochalski, J. (2007). International nurse migration: Lessons from the Philippines. *Policy, Politics, & Nursing Practice*, 8(1), 37–46.

Buchan, J., Campbell, J., Dhillon, I. & Charlesworth, A. (2019). Labour market change and the international mobility of health workers. *Health Foundation Working Paper*, 5.

Buchan, J., Catton, H. & Shaffer, F. A. (2022). *Sustain and retain in 2022 and beyond: The global nursing workforce and the Covid-19 pandemic*. Geneva: International Centre on Nursing Migration.

Bureau of International Organization Affairs & Office of United Nations Political Affairs. (1989). *Trust territory of the Pacific Islands*. Berkely, CA: University of California.

Cabanda, E. (2020). "We want your nurses!": Negotiating labor agreements in recruiting Filipino nurses. *Asian Politics & Policy*, 12(3), 404–431.

Campbell, J. (2018). *SDG3.c1 health worker density and distribution: Health worker labour mobility*. World Health Organization: Health Workforce Department.

Canadian Medical Association Journal (CMAJ). (2010). Portuguese-speaking African countries face shortages of doctors. *CMAJ*, 182(11), E511–E512. www.cmaj.ca/content/cmaj/182/11/E511.full.pdf.

Castro-Palaganas, E., Spitzer, D. L., Kabamalan, M. M. M. et al. (2017). An examination of the causes, consequences, and policy responses to the migration of highly trained health personnel from the Philippines: The high cost of living/leaving – a mixed method study. *Human Resources for Health*, 15(1), 1–14.

Chad – Higher Education. (n.d.). https://education.stateuniversity.com/pages/257/Chad-HIGHER-EDUCATION.html.

Chatzidakis, A., Hakim, J., Litter, J. & Rottenberg, C. (2020). *The care manifesto: The politics of interdependence*. London: Verso Books.

Chikanda, A. (2006). Skilled health professionals' migration and its impact on health delivery in Zimbabwe. *Journal of Ethnic and Migration Studies*, 32 (04), 667–680.

Chikanda, A. (2022). Migration intermediaries and the migration of health professionals from the global South. In M. Walton-Roberts, eds., *Global Migration, Gender and Health Professional Credentials: Transnational Value Transfers and Losses*. Toronto: University of Toronto Press, pp. 167–186.

Choi, S. & Lyons, L. (2012). Gender, citizenship, and women's "unskilled" labour: The experience of Filipino migrant nurses in Singapore. *Canadian Journal of Women and the Law*, 24(1), 1–26.

Choy, C. C. (2003). *Empire of care*. Durham NC: Duke University Press.

Clark, P. F., Stewart, J. B. & Clark, D. A. (2006). The globalization of the labour market for health-care professionals. *International Labour Review*, 145(1–2), 37–64.

Clemens, M. A. (2015). Global skill partnerships: A proposal for technical training in a mobile world. *IZA Journal of Labor Policy*, 4(1), 1–18.

Clemens, M. A. & Dempster, H. (2021). *Ethical recruitment of health workers: Using bilateral cooperation to fulfill the World Health Organization's global code of practice*. Center for Global Development. Policy Paper 212.

Coffey, C., Espinoza Revollo, P., Harvey, R. et al. (2020). *Time to care: Unpaid and underpaid care work and the global inequality crisis*. Oxford: Oxfam International.

Connell, J. (2008). Niue: Embracing a culture of migration. *Journal of Ethnic and Migration Studies*, 34(6), 1021–1040, https://doi.10.1080/1369183080 2211315.

Connell, J. (2010a). Pacific islands in the global economy: Paradoxes of migration and culture. *Singapore Journal of Tropical Geography*, 31(1), 115–129.

Connell, J. (2010b). *Migration of health workers in the Asia-Pacific region*. Sydney: Human Resources for Health Knowledge Hub, University of New South Wales.

Connell, J. (2014). The two cultures of health worker migration: A Pacific perspective. *Social Science & Medicine*, 116, 73–81.

Connell, J. & Buchan, J. (2011). The impossible dream? Codes of practice and the international migration of skilled health workers. *World Medical & Health Policy*, 3(3), 1–17.

Connell, J. & Stilwell, B. (2006) Merchants of medical care: Recruiting agencies in the global health care chain. Merchants of Labour. *International Institute for Labour Studies*, IV, 239–253.

Connell, J. & Walton-Roberts, M. (2016). What about the workers? The missing geographies of health care. *Progress in Human Geography*, 40(2), 158–176.

Cowan, D. & Wilson-Barnett, J. (2006). European healthcare training and accreditation network (EHTAN) project. *International Journal of Nursing Studies*, 43(3), 265–267.

Crone, R. (2008). Flat medicine? Exploring trends in the globalization of health care. *Academic Medicine*, 83(2), 117–121.

Crush, J. (2022). Peripatetic physicians: Rewriting the South African brain drain narrative. In M. Walton-Roberts, ed., *Global Migration, Gender, and Health Professional Credentials*. Toronto: University of Toronto Press, pp. 326–346.

Crush, J., Chikanda, A. & Tawodzera, G. (2015). The third wave: Mixed migration from Zimbabwe to South Africa. *Canadian Journal of African Studies/Revue canadienne des études africaines*, 49(2), 363–382.

Daniels, J. P. (2020). Venezuelan migrants "struggling to survive" amid COVID-19. *The Lancet*, 395(10229), 1023.

De Haas, H., Castles, S. & Miller, M. J. (2019). *The age of migration: International population movements in the modern world*. Bloomsbury. London: Bloomsbury Academic.

De Silva, M. (2017). The care pentagon: Older adults within Sri Lankan-Australian transnational families and their landscapes of care. *Population, Space and Place*, 23(8), 1–9.

Dhillon, I. S., Clark, M. E. & Kapp, R. H. (2010). A guidebook on bilateral agreements to address health worker migration. Washington, DC: Aspen Institute.

Directorate General for Foreign Trade, Belize. (2021). *Trade in health services: Nurses*. www.dgft.gov.bz/trade-in-health-services-nurses/.

Docquier, F. & Rapoport, H. (2012). Globalization, brain drain, and development. *Journal of Economic Literature*, 50(3), 681–730.

Eaton, M. (2003). Portugal's lusophone African immigrants: Colonial legacy in a contemporary labour market. In S. Lloyd-Jones & A. Costa Pinto, eds., *The Last Empire: Thirty Years of Portuguese Decolonization*. Bristol: Intellect, pp. 99–111.

Efendi, F., Haryanto, J., Indarwati, R. et al. (2021). Going global: Insights of Indonesian policymakers on international migration of nurses. *Journal of Multidisciplinary Healthcare*, 14, 3285–3293.

Ennis, C. A. & Walton-Roberts, M. (2018). Labour market regulation as global social policy: The case of nursing labour markets in Oman. *Global Social Policy*, 18(2), 169–188.

European Commission. (2021). *The state of health in the EU: Companion report 2021*. The European Commission's Directorate-General for Health and Food Safety. https://ec.europa.eu/health/state-health-eu/country-health-profiles_en.

Eurostat Health Care Staff. (2021). *Health workforce migration*. https://ec .europa.eu/eurostat/cache/metadata/Annexes/hlth_res_esms_an13.pdf.

Fihlani, P. (2016). Namibia's "home-grown doctors" start to make a difference. *BBC News*, Africa. November 1. www.bbc.com/news/world-africa-37780777.

Fineman, M. A. (2008). The vulnerable subject: Anchoring equality in the human condition. *Yale JL & Feminism*, 20, 1–23.

Fisher, B. & Tronto, J. (1990). Toward a feminist theory of caring. In E. Abel & M. Nelson, eds., *Circles of Care: Work and Identity in Women's Lives*. Albany, NY: State University of New York Press, pp. 35–62.

Fronteira, I., Sidat, M., Fresta, M. et al. (2014). The rise of medical training in Portuguese speaking African countries. *Human Resources for Health*, 12(63, 1–10). https://doi.org/10.1186/1478-4491-12-.

Fukunaga, Y. (2015). *Assessing the progress of ASEAN MRAs on professional services*. Economic Research Institute for ASEAN and East Asia Discussion Paper 21.

Gabriel, C. (2013). NAFTA, skilled migration, and continental nursing markets. *Population, Space and Place*, 19(4), 389–403.

George, S. (2005). *When women come first: Gender and class in transnational migration*. Oakland: University of California Press.

George, G. & Rhodes, B. (2017). Is there a financial incentive to immigrate? Examining of the health worker salary gap between India and popular destination countries. *Human Resources for Health*, 15(1), 1–10.

Ghosh, B. (2019). Health workforce development planning in the Sultanate of Oman: A case study. *Human Resources for Health*, 7(47), 1–15.

Gibson, J. & McKenzie, D. (2011). Eight questions about brain drain. *Journal of Economic Perspectives*, 25(3), 107–128.

Gootiiz, B. & Mattoo, A. (2017). Regionalism in services: A study of ASEAN. *The World Economy*, 40(3), 574–597.

Government of Canada. (2021). *Government of Canada announces recipients of $100-million feminist response and recovery fund*. Women and Gender Equality Canada News Release. July 29.

Government of Ontario. (2019). *Annual report of the office of the fairness commissioner: 2018–2019*. Office of the Fairness Commissioner. March 31. www.fairnesscommissioner.ca/en/Publications/PDF/Annual% 20Reports/OFC_Annual_Report_2018-2019.pdf.

Hagander, L. E., Hughes, C. D., Nash, K. et al. (2013). Surgeon migration between developing countries and the United States: Train, retain, and gain from brain drain. *World Journal of Surgery*, 37(1), 14–23.

Hammett, D. (2014). Physician migration in the global South between Cuba and South Africa. *International Migration*, 52(4), 41–52.

Harden, R. M. (2006). International medical education and future directions: A global perspective. *Academic Medicine*, 81(12), S22–S29.

Hart, J. T. (1971). The inverse care law. *The Lancet*, 297(7696), 405–412.

Hawthorne, L. (2010). Two-step migration: Australia's experience. POLICY, pp. 39–43.

Hawthorne, L. (2015). *International health workforce mobility and its implications in the Western Pacific region*. Melbourne School of Population and Global Health. https://minerva-access.unimelb.edu.au/bitstream/handle/11343/208881/ 2015%20WHOAsiaHealthWorkforceMobility16AugustVeryFinal.pdf.

Healey, M. (2010). "Regarded, paid and housed as menials": Nursing in colonial India, 1900–1948. *South Asian History and Culture*, 2(1), 55–75.

Hillman, F., Walton-Roberts, M. & Yeoh, B. (2022). Moving nurses to cities: On how migration industries feed into global urban assemblages in the care sector. *Urban Studies*, 59(11), 2294–2312.

HM Treasury. (2021). *Build back better: Our plan for growth*. APS Group on behalf of the Controller of Her Majesty's Stationery Office Policy Paper 03/ 21. March 3.

Hochschild, A. R. (2000). The nanny chain. *American Prospect*, 11(4), 32–36.

Hodal, K. (2012). Cuban infusion remains the lifeblood of Timor-Leste's health service. *The Guardian*, Europe. www.theguardian.com/global-development/ 2012/jun/25/cuba-lifeblood-timor-leste-health-service.

Hogan, S. (2020). Florence Nightingale (1820–1910)–what does history say about her feminism? *Journal of Gender Studies*, 30(8), 915–926.

Hudson-Sharp, N., Runge, J. & Rolfe, H. (2017). *Use of agency workers in the public sector*. National Institute of Economic and Social Research Report. February 20. www.niesr.ac.uk/publications/use-agency-workers-public-sector.

International Council of Nurses (ICN). (2021). *Nursing action and impact in global health policy making*. ICN Report 74th World Health Assembly. July 27.

International Federation for Emergency Medicine (IFEM). (2020). *Dr Lisa Charles shares her story of life as an emergency medicine physician in Saint Lucia*. January 27.

International Labour Organization (ILO). (2021). *Building forward fairer: Women's rights to work and at work at the core of the COVID-19 recovery.* ILO Policy Brief. July 19.

Itaki, R. (2020). Small pacific island countries contiune to struggle with lack of doctors and nurses. *Pacific Family Health Journal.* https://pacific-family-health.com/2020/10/02/small-pacific-island-countries-continue-to-struggle-with-lack-of-doctors-and-nurses/.

Jafri, N. (2022). Ten years of Ontario's fair-access law: Has access to regulated professions improved for internationally educated individuals? In M. Walton-Roberts, ed., *Global Migration, Gender, and Health Professional Credentials.* Toronto: University of Toronto Press, pp. 230–245.

Jarman, H. & Greer, S. (2010). Crossborder trade in health services: Lessons from the European laboratory. *Health Policy,* 94(2), 158–163.

Jung, Y. S. (2018). Beyond the bifurcated myth: The medical migration of female korean nurses to West Germany in the 1970s. *Korean Journal of Medical History,* 27(2), 225–266.

Kallström, A., Al-Abdulla, O., Parkki, J. et al. (2021). I had to leave. I had to leave my clinic, my city, leave everything behind in Syria. Qualitative research of Syrian healthcare workers migrating from the war-torn country. *BMJ Open,* 11(11), 1–8.

Karapetyan, S. (2019). *Association seeks to empower doctors in Seychelles through training, better work conditions.* Seychelles News Agency. July 2.

Kasuba, R. & Ziliukas, P. (2004). A comparative review of two major international accrediting consortia for engineering education: The Washington accord and the Bologna process. *World Transactions on Engineering and Technology Education,* 1(1), 71–74.

Kennedy Center for International Studies. (2022). *Thailand health care.* Brigham Young University.

Kingma, M. (2006). *Nurses on the Move: Migration and the global health care economy.* Ithaca, NY: Cornell University Press.

Kline, D. S. (2003). Push and pull factors in international nurse migration. *Journal of Nursing Scholarship,* 35(2), 107–111.

Koehn, P. H. (2006). Globalization, migration health, and educational preparation for transnational medical encounters. *Globalization and Health,* 2(1), 1–16.

Kronfol, N. M., Sibai, A. M. & Rafeh, N. (1992). The impact of civil disturbances on the migration of physicians: The case of Lebanon. *Medical Care,* 30 (3), 208–215.

Kwete, X., Tang, K., Chen, L. et al. (2022). Decolonizing global health: What should be the target of this movement and where does it lead us? *Global Health Research and Policy,* 7(1), 1–6.

Labonté, R., Sanders, D., Mathole, T. et al. (2015). Health worker migration from South Africa: Causes, consequences and policy responses. *Human Resources for Health*, 13(1), 1–16.

Levitt, P. & Rajaram, N. (2013). Moving toward reform? Mobility, health, and development in the context of neoliberalism. *Migration Studies*, 1(3), 338–362.

Lewis, S. (2006). *Race against time: Searching for hope in AIDS-ravaged Africa*. Toronto: House of Anansi Press.

Linder, R. (2021). Israel has abandoned medical training. This is what it can do fix it. *Haaretz, Israel News*. July 13. www.haaretz.com/israel-news/.pre mium-israel-has abandoned-medical-training-this-is-what-it-can-do-fix-it-1.9996105.

Lorenzo, F. M. E., Galvez-Tan, J., Icamina, K. & Javier, L. (2007). Nurse migration from a source country perspective: Philippine country case study. *Health Services Research*, 42(3p2), 1406–1418.

Lotta, G., Fernandez, M., Pimenta, D. & Wenham, C. (2021). Gender, race, and health workers in the COVID-19 pandemic. *The Lancet*, 397(10281), 1264.

Luska Times. (2018). Calibre of medical doctors trained abroad questioned. January 15. www.lusakatimes.com/2018/01/15/calibre-medical-doctors-trained-abroad-questioned/.

Mackey, T. K. & Liang, B. A. (2012). Rebalancing brain drain: Exploring resource reallocation to address health worker migration and promote global health. *Health Policy*, 107(1), 66–73.

Mackintosh, M., Raghuram, P. & Henry, L. (2006). A perverse subsidy: African trained nurses and doctors in the NHS. *Soundings*, 34(34), 103–113.

Macklin, A. (1991). Foreign domestic worker: Surrogate housewife or mail order servant. *McGill Law Journal*, 37(3), 681–760.

MacReady, N. (2007). Developing countries court medical tourists. *The Lancet*, 369(9576), 1849–1850.

Main, I. (2020). *Nurses in Poland, migration and the pandemic*. Migration for Welfare. December 4.

Manyisa, Z. M. & van Aswegen, E. J. (2017). Factors affecting working conditions in public hospitals: A literature review. *International Journal of Africa Nursing Sciences*, 6, 28–38.

Masselink, L. E. & Lee, S. Y. D. (2010). Nurses, Inc.: Expansion and commercialization of nursing education in the Philippines. *Social Science & Medicine*, 71(1), 166–172.

Martineau, T., Decker, K. & Bundred, P. (2002). *Briefing note on international migration of health professionals: Levelling the playing field for developing country health systems*. Liverpool: Liverpool School of Tropical Medicine.

Mauldin, L. (2022). The care crisis isn't what you think: Our problems are deeper than a lack of care infrastructure. *The American Prospect*. January 3.

McDonald, L. (2010). *Florence nightingale at first hand: Vision, power, legacy*. London: Bloomsbury Academic.

McQuide, P. A., Kolehmainen-Aitken, R. L. & Forster, N. (2013). Applying the workload indicators of staffing need (WISN) method in Namibia: Challenges and implications for human resources for health policy. *Human Resources for Health*, 11, 1–11. https://doi.org/10.1186/1478-4491-11-64.

Meeks, G. W. (2021). The build back better world partnership could finally break the belt and road. *Foreign Policy*. June 28.

Mejia, A., Pizurki, H. & Royston, E. (1979). *Physician and nurse migrant: Analysis and policy implications*. Geneva: World Health Organisation.

Minority Nurse. (2013). *Professional nursing in Oman*. March 30. https://minoritynurse.com/professional-nursing-in-oman/.

Morgan, J., Crooks, V. A. & Snyder, J. (2017). "We have been forced to move away from home": Print news coverage of Canadians studying abroad at Caribbean offshore medical schools. *BMC Medical Education*, 17(1), 1–9.

Morgan, J., Crooks, V., Snyder, J. & Pickering, J. (2018). "They don't have the history and the stature": Examining perceptions of Caribbean offshore medical schools held by Canadian medical education stakeholders. *Canadian Medical Education Journal*, 9(3), e56–e63.

Mullally, S. & Wright, D. (2020). *Foreign practices: Immigrant doctors and the history of Canadian medicare*. Montreal: McGill-Queens University Press.

Naiki, Y. (2015). Labour migration under the Japan-Philippines and Japan-Indonesia economic partnership agreements. In M. Panizzon, G. Zürcher & E. Fornalé, eds., *The Palgrave Handbook of International Labour Migration*. London: Palgrave Macmillan, pp. 341–358.

National Health Workforce Accounts Data Portal (n.d). https://apps.who.int/nhwaportal/.

National Reporting Instrument Reports Database (2018). World Health Organization. Geneva. www.who.int/hrh/migration/code/code_nri/reports.

Nolan, S. (2022). Rich countries lure health workers from low-income nations to fight shortages. *New York Times, Health*. January 24. www.nytimes.com/2022/01/24/health/covid-health-worker-immigration.html.

Ochiai, E. (2009). Care diamonds and welfare regimes in East and South-East Asian societies: Bridging family and welfare sociology. *International Journal of Japanese Sociology*, 18(1), 60–78.

Oda, H., Tsujita, Y. & Irudaya Rajan, S. (2018). An analysis of factors influencing the international migration of Indian nurses. *Journal of International Migration and Integration*, 19(3), 607–624.

Olds, R. (2016). Reversing the medical brain drain. *The Jordan Times*. November 28. https://jordantimes.com/opinion/g-richard-olds/reversing-medical-brain-drain.

Oman Ministry of Health. *Directorate of Nursing and Midwifery Affairs: Services*.

Organisation for Economic Co-operation and Development (OECD). (2020). *Contribution of migrant doctors and nurses to tackling COVID-19 crisis in OECD countries*.

Ormond, M. (2020). International medical travel, or medical tourism. In A. Kobayashi, ed., *International Encyclopedia of Human Geography*. London: Elsevier BV, pp. 373–377.

Ormond, M. & Toyota, M. (2018). Transnationalizing the provision of care. "Rethinking care through transnational health and long-term care practices". In V. A. Crooks, J. Pearce & G. Andrews, eds., *Routledge Handbook of Health Geography*. Abingdon: Routledge, pp. 237–243.

Ortiga, Y. Y. (2018a). Learning to fill the labor niche: Filipino nursing graduates and the risk of the migration trap. *RSF: The Russell Sage Foundation Journal of the Social Sciences*, 4(1), 172–187.

Ortiga, Y. Y. (2018b). *Emigration, employability and higher education in the Philippines*. New York: Routledge.

Ortiga, Y. Y., Wee, K. & Yeoh, B. S. (2021). Connecting care chains and care diamonds: The elderly care skills regime in Singapore. *Global Networks*, 21(2), 434–454.

Packer, C., Labonté, R. & Runnels, V. (2009). Globalization and the cross-border flow of health workers. In *Globalization and Health*. NY: Routledge, pp. 235–256.

Paul, A. M. & Yeoh, B. S. (2021). Studying multinational migrations, speaking back to migration theory. *Global Networks*, 21(1), 3–17.

Parreñas, R. S. (2000). Migrant Filipina domestic workers and the international division of reproductive labor. *Gender & Society*, 14(4), 560–580.

Pasternak, D. P. & Chen, B. (2016). *Primary source verification of health care professionals: A risk reduction strategy for patients and health care organizations*. White Paper. Joint Commission International.

Peng, I. (2018). Shaping and reshaping care and migration in East and Southeast Asia. *Critical Sociology*, 44(7–8), 1117–1132 (online first).

Percot, M. (2006). Indian nurses in the Gulf: Two generations of female migration. *South Asia Research*, 26(1), 41–62.

Persaud, D., Cole, J., Jainarine, R. & Khalid, Z. (2017). Internal medicine residency program in Guyana: A collaborative model for sustainable graduate medical education in resource-limited settings. *Frontiers in Public Health*, 5, 1–9. https://doi.org/10.3389/fpubh.2017.00112.

Picot, G. & Sweetman, A. (2011). *Canadian immigration policy and immigrant economic outcomes: Why the differences in outcomes between Sweden and Canada?* Bonn: Institute for the Study of Labor.

Pierantozzi, S. S. (2005). Status of public health in the Republic of Palau. *Pacific Health Dialog*, 12(1), 11–13.

Pointe, E. (2020). *International year of nurses and midwives.* Seychelles Nation: Health.

Pope, L. (2018). *Seychelles nurses advance their education at Chamberlain.* Addison, IL: Chamberlain University.

Raghuram, P. (2012). Global care, local configurations–challenges to concep-tualizations of care. *Global Networks*, 12(2), 155–174.

Raghuram, P, Bornat, J. & Henry, L. (2011). The co-marking of aged bodies and migrant bodies: Migrant workers' contribution to geriatric medicine in the UK. *Sociology of Health & Illness*, 33(2), 321–335.

Rafferty, A. M. & Solano, D. (2007). The rise and demise of the colonial nursing service: British nurses in the colonies, 1896–1966. *Nursing History Review*, 15(1), 147–154.

Reddy, S. K. (2015). *Nursing and empire: Gendered labor and migration from India to the United States.* Chapel Hill: UNC Press Books.

Reinalda, B. (2008). The Bologna process and its achievements in Europe 1999–2007. *Journal of Political Science Education*, 4(4), 463–476.

The Report: Oman. (2017). N.p.: Oxford Business Group. 242–4.

Riley, P. L., Zuber, A., Vindigni, S. M. et al. (2012). Information systems on human resources for health: A global review. *Human Resources for Health*, 10(1), 1–12.

Rodriguez, R. M. (2010). *Migrants for export: How the Philippine state brokers labor to the world.* Minnesota: University of Minnesota Press.

Ruhs, M. & Anderson, B. (2013). Responding to employers: Skills, shortages and sensible immigration policy. In G. Brochmann & E. Jurado, eds., *Europe's Immigration Challenge: Reconciling Work, Welfare and Mobility.* London: I.B. Tauris, pp. 95–104.

Sammie, A. (2014). *Senator calls for medical training in Saint Lucia.* Government of Saint Lucia. September 14. www.govt.lc/news/senator-calls-for-medical-training-in-saint-lucia.

Sasikumar, S. K. & Thimothy, R. (2015). *From India to the Gulf region: Exploring links between labour markets, skills and the migration cycle.* Deutsche Gesellschaft fur Internationale (GIZ) and International Labour Organisation (ILO). www.ilo.org/newdelhi/whatwedo/publications/WCMS_397363/lang–en/index.htm.

Saudi Gazette. (2018). *Nearly 6,000 Saudi doctors without jobs*. July 28. https://saudigazette.com.sa/article/539964.

Scheffler, R. M., Campbell, J., Cometto, G. et al. (2018). Forecasting imbalances in the global health labor market and devising policy responses. *Human Resources for Health*, 16(1), 1–10.

Schumacher, P. & Leung, M. (2018). Knowledge (im) mobility through mirco-level interactions: An analysis of the communication process in Chinese-Zambian medical co-operation. *Transnational Social Review*, 8(1), 64–78.

Schwiter, K., Brütsch, J. & Pratt, G. (2020). Sending granny to Chiang Mai: Debating global outsourcing of care for the elderly. *Global Networks*, 20(1), 106–125.

Segouin, C., Hodges, B. & Brechat, P. H. (2005). Globalization in health care: Is international standardization of quality a step toward outsourcing? *IJQHC: International Journal for Quality in Health Care*, 17(4), 277–279.

Shaffer, F. A., Bakhshi, M. A., Farrell, N. & Álvarez, T. D. (2020). CE: Original research: The recruitment experience of foreign-educated health professionals to the United States. *AJN: The American Journal of Nursing*, 120(1), 28–38.

Sheel, M. & Rendell, N. (2022). *Health security in the Pacific: Expert perspectives to guide health system strengthening*. University of Sydney. https://ses.library.usyd.edu.au/handle/2123/28200.

Sikorski, T. M. (1994). Limits to financial liberalization: The experiences of Indonesia and the Philippines. *Savings and Development*, 18(4), 393–426. https://www.jstor.org/stable/25830393?seq=1.

Smith, R. D., Chanda, R. & Tangcharoensathien, V. (2009). Trade in health-related services. *The Lancet*, 373(9663), 593–601.

Stephenson, S. & Hufbauer, G. (2011). Labor mobility. In J. P. Chauffour & J. C. Maur, eds., *Preferential Trade Agreement Policies for Development: A Handbook*. Washington, DC: World Bank, pp. 275–306.

Stilwell, B., Diallo, K., Zurn, P. et al. (2004). Migration of health-care workers from developing countries: strategic approaches to its management. *Bulletin of the World Health Organization*, 82, 595–600.

Sufi, Q. (2013). *First group of qualified Chadians from France Arrive in Chad*. IOM UN Migration. Feburary 19.

Sweetman, A. (2022). The migration of health professionals to Canada: Reducing brain waste and improving labour market integration. In M. Walton-Roberts, ed., *Global Migration, Gender, and Health Professional Credentials*. Toronto: University of Toronto Press, pp. 71–94.

Sweetman, A., McDonald, J. T. & Hawthorne, L. (2015). Occupational regulation and foreign qualification recognition: An overview. *Canadian Public Policy*, 41(Supplement 1), S1–S13.

Tangcharoensathien, V., Travis, P., Tancarino, A. S. et al. (2018). Managing in- and out migration of health workforce in selected countries in South East Asia region. *International Journal of Health Policy and Medicine*, 7(2), 137–143. http://doi.10.15171/ijhpm.2017.49.

Taylor, A. L. & Dhillon, I. S. (2011). The WHO global code of practice on the international recruitment of health personnel: The evolution of global health diplomacy. *Global Health Governance*, 5(1), 1–24.

Te, V., Griffiths, R., Law, K., Hill, P. S. & Annear, P. L. (2018). The impact of ASEAN economic integration on health worker mobility: A scoping review of the literature. *Health Policy and Planning*, 33(8), 957–965.

Thompson, M. & Walton-Roberts, M. (2019). International nurse migration from India and the Philippines: The challenge of meeting the sustainable development goals in training, orderly migration and healthcare worker retention. *Journal of Ethnic and Migration Studies*, 45(14), 2583–2599.

Thorlby, R., Gardner, T., Everest, G. et al. (2021). *The health foundation the NHS long term plan and COVID-19*. London: The Health Foundation.

Timmons, S., Evans, C. & Nair, S. (2016). The development of the nursing profession in a globalised context: A qualitative case study in Kerala, India. *Social Science & Medicine*, 166, 41–48.

Tobgay, T., Dorji, T., Pelzom, D. & Gibbons, R. V. (2011). Progress and delivery of health care in Bhutan, the land of the thunder dragon and gross national happiness. *Tropical Medicine & International Health*, 16(6), 731–736. https://doi.org/10.1111/j.1365-3156.2011.02760.x.

Tomblin-Murphy, G., MacKenzie, A., Waysome, B. et al. (2016). A mixed-methods study of health worker migration from Jamaica. *Human Resources for Health*, 14(1), 89–103.

Torresan, A. (2021). Postcolonial social drama: The case of Brazilian dentists in Portugal. *Critique of Anthropology*, 41(2), 165–186.

Tronto, J. C. (1998). An ethic of care. *Generations: Journal of the American Society on Aging*, 22(3), 15–20.

Türegün, A. (2017). Ideas and interests embedded in the making of Ontario's fair access to regulated professions act, 2006. *International Migration & Integration*, 18, 405–418. https://doi.org/10.1007/s12134-016-0506-9.

United Nations Economic and Social Commission for Asia and the Pacific. (2021). *COVID-19 and the unpaid care economy in Asia and the Pacific*. Regional Report. September 9.

United Nations General Assembly (UNGA). (2018). *Global compact for safe, orderly and regular migration: Resolution adopted by the general assembly on 19 December 2018*. Report. A/RES/73/195. www.un.org/en/ga/search/view_doc.asp?symbol=A/RES/73/195.

Valiani, S. (2011). *Rethinking unequal exchange: The Global Integration of Nursing Labour Markets*. Toronto: University of Toronto Press.

Van den Broek, D. & Groutsis, D. (2017). Global nursing and the lived experience of migration intermediaries. *Work, Employment and Society*, 31(5), 851–860.

Van den Broek, D., Harvey, W. & Groutsis, D. (2016). Commercial migration intermediaries and the segmentation of skilled migrant employment. *Work, Employment and Society*, 30(3), 523–534.

Van Hear, N., Bakewell, O. & Long, K. (2018). Push-pull plus: Reconsidering the drivers of migration. *Journal of Ethnic and Migration Studies*, 44(6), 927–944.

Varga, J. (2017). Out-migration and attrition of physicians and dentists before and after EU accession (2003 and 2011): The case of Hungary. *European Journal of Health Economics*, 18(9), 1079–1093. https://doi.org/10.1007/s10198-016-0854-6.

Varghese, V. J. (2020). An industry of frauds? State policy, migration assemblages and nursing professionals from India. In M. Baas, ed., *The Migration Industry in Asia, Palgrave Pivot*. Singapore: Palgrave Macmillan, pp. 109–133.

Walton-Roberts, M. (2012) Contextualizing the global nurse care chain: International migration and the status of nursing in south India. *Global Networks*, 12(2), 175–194.

Walton-Roberts, M. (2014). European education regionalization and its influence on the global migration of nurses. In M. Walton-Roberts & J. Hennebry, eds., *Territoriality and Migration Management in the E.U. Neighbourhood. Spilling over the Wall*. New York: Springer International Migration Series, pp. 49–64.

Walton-Roberts, M. (2015a). The international migration of health professionals and the marketization and privatization of health education in India: From push-pull to global political economy. *Social Science and Medicine*, 124, 374–382.

Walton-Roberts, M. (2015b). Migration: The mobility of patients and health professionals. In N. Lunt, D. Horsfall & J. Hanefeld, eds., *Handbook on Medical Tourism and Patient Mobility*. Cheltenham: Edward Elgar, pp. 238–246.

Walton-Roberts, M. (2015c). Transnational health institutions, global nursing care chains, and the internationalization of nurse education in Punjab. In S. I. Rajan, V. J. Varghese & A. K. Nanda, eds., *Migrations, Mobility and Multiple Affiliations: Punjabis in a Transnational World*. Delhi: Cambridge University Press, pp. 296–316.

Walton-Roberts, M. (2020a). Occupational (im) mobility in the global care economy: The case of foreign-trained nurses in the Canadian context. *Journal of Ethnic and Migration Studies*, 46(16), 3441–3456.

Walton-Roberts, M. (2020b). The production of nurses for global markets: Tracing capital and labour circulation in and out of Asia. In P. Aulakh & P. F. Kelly, eds., *Asian Connections: Linking Mobilities of Labour and Capital*. Cambridge: Cambridge University Press, pp. 211–232.

Walton-Roberts, M. (2021). Bus stops, triple wins and two steps: Nurse migration in and out of Asia. *Global Networks*, 21(1), 84–107.

Walton-Roberts, M., Bhutani, S. & Kaur, A. (2017a). Care and global migration in the nursing profession: A north Indian perspective. *Australian Geographer*, 48(1), 59–77.

Walton-Roberts, M., Runnels, V., Rajan, I. S. et al. (2017b). Causes, consequences and policy responses to the migration of health workers: Key findings from India. *Human Resources for Health*, 15(28), 1–18.

Walton-Roberts, M. & Khadria, B. (2023). "Friendly relations" in the troubled time: Tracing a decade of nurse migration from India to the UAE. In R. Adhikari & E. Plotnikova, eds., *Nurse Migration in Asia*. New York: Routledge, pp. 36–52.

Walton-Roberts, M. & Rajan, S. I. (2020). Global demand for medical professionals drives Indians abroad despite acute domestic health-care worker shortages. *Migration Policy Institute (MPI)*. www.migrationpolicy.org/art icle/global-demand-medical-professionals-drives-indians-abroad.

Walton-Roberts, M., Rajan, S. I. & Joseph, J. (2022). Gendered mobility and multi-scaler governance models: Exploring the case of nurse migration from India to the Gulf. In C. Ennis & N. Blarel, eds., *The South Asia to Gulf Migration Governance Complex*. Bristol: Bristol University Press, pp. 35–55.

White House. (2021). The build back better framework: President biden's plan to rebuild the Middle Class. www.whitehouse.gov/build-back-better/.

Wickramasekara, P. (2012). Something is better than nothing: Enhancing the protection of Indian migrant workers through bilateral agreements and memoranda of understanding. *SSRN Electronic Journal*, 1–49. https://doi .org/10.2139/ssrn.2032136.

Wiskow, C. (2006). *Health worker migration flows in Europe: Overview and case studies in selected CEE countries-Romania, Czech Republic, Serbia and Croatia*. International Labour Organization.

WHO. (2002). *Ethical choices in long-term care: What does justice require?* Geneva: World Health Organization. www.who.int/mediacentre/news/notes/ ethical_choices.pdf.

WHO. (2006). *The world health report: 2006 : Working together for health.* Geneva: World Health Organization. https://apps.who.int/iris/handle/10665/43432.

WHO. (2010a). *International migration of health workers improving international co-operation to address the global health workforce crisis*, OECD Policy Brief, Paris: OECD.

WHO. (2010b). *WHO global code of practice on the international recruitment of health personnel.* Geneva: World Health Organization. www.who.int/hrh/migration/code/WHO_global_code_of_practice_EN.pdf.

WHO. (2016a). *Global strategy on human resources for health: Workforce 2030.* Geneva: World Health Organization.

WHO. (2016b). Health workforce requirements for universal health coverage and the sustainable development goals. *Human resources for health observer, 17.*

WHO. (2017a). *A dynamic understanding of health worker migration.* www.who.int/hrh/HWF17002_Brochure.pdf.

WHO. (2017b). *Women on the Move: Migration, care work, and health.* Geneva: World Health Organization.

WHO. (2017c). *Country cooperation strategy Kuwait.* Accessed October 16, 2022. http://apps.who.int/iris/bitstream/handle/10665/136906/ccsbrief_kwt_en.pdf.

WHO. (2018). *Understanding national health workforce accounts.* Report No. WHO/HIS/HWF/NHWA/2017.1. Geneva: World Health Organization.

WHO. (2020a). *WHO and European investment bank strengthen efforts to combat COVID-19 and build resilient health systems to face future pandemics.* News Release. May 01. www.whitehouse.gov/build-back-better/.

WHO. (2020b). *Report of the WHO expert advisory group on the relevance and effectiveness of the WHO global code of practice on the international recruitment of health personnel.* Report A73/9. 73rd World Health Assembly. May 8. https://apps.who.int/gb/ebwha/pdf_files/WHA73/A73_9-en.pdf.

WHO. (2020c). *Postgraduate training in Monaco.* https://apps.who.int/iris/bitstream/handle/10665/336241/WHO-EURO-2020-1307-41057-55737-eng.pdf?sequence=1&isAllowed=y.

WHO. (2021a). *COVID-19 and measures to "build back better" essential health services to achieve UHC and the health related SDGs.* Regional Office for South-East Asia SEA/RC74/3. September 10.

WHO. (2021b). *COVID-19 response capacity with the health system: Health workforce recruitment and retention.* Regional Office for Africa Rapid Policy Brief Number: 011–03. Brazzaville: Licence: CC BY-NC-SA 3.0 IGO. December 31.

WHO. (2021c). *Health workforce support and safeguards list, 2020.* Geneva: World Health Organization. https://cdn.who.int/media/docs/default-source/health-workforce/hwf-support-and-safeguards-list8jan.pdf?sfvrsn=1a16bc6f_14.

Xiang, B. & Lindquist, J. (2014). Migration infrastructure. *International Migration Review*, 48(1_suppl), 122–148.

Yang, P. (2018). Compromise and complicity in international student mobility: The ethnographic case of Indian medical students at a Chinese university. *Discourse: Studies in the Cultural Politics of Education*, 39(5), 694–708.

Yeates, N. (2009). *Globalising care economies and migrant workers: Explorations in global care chains.* Houndmills: Palgrave Macmillan

Yeates, N. (2011). Going global: The transnationalization of care. *Development and Change*, 42(4), 1109–1130.

Yeates, N. & Pillinger, J. (2019). *International health worker migration and recruitment: Global governance, politics and policy.* London: Routledge.

Yeoh, B. S. & Huang, S. (2015). Cosmopolitan beginnings? Transnational healthcare workers and the politics of carework in Singapore. *The Geographical Journal*, 181(3), 249–258.

Yeoh, B. S. & Huang, S. (2014). Singapore's changing demography, the elder-care predicament and transnational "care" migration. *TraNS: Trans-Regional and-National Studies of Southeast Asia*, 2(2), 247–269.

Yeoh, B. S. & Lam, T. (2016). Immigration and its (dis) contents: The challenges of highly skilled migration in globalizing Singapore. *American Behavioral Scientist*, 60(5–6), 637–658.

Zawawi, A. N. & Al-Rashed, A. M. (2020). The experiences of foreign doctors in Saudi Arabia: A qualitative study of the challenges and retention motives. *Science Direct*, 6(8), 1–9. https://doi.org/10.1016/j.heliyon.2020.e03901.

Acknowledgement

This book draws upon research that was funded by the Social Sciences and Humanities Research Council of Canada grant number 435-2019-0687. I would like to thank Peter Ho and the Cambridge University Press team and two peer reviewers for their feedback. I would also like to thank Alicia Pouw and Samatha Zani for their valuable research assistance.

Cambridge Elements ⚌

Global Development Studies

Peter Ho
Zhejiang University

Peter Ho is Distinguished Professor at Zhejiang University and high-level National Expert of China. He has held or holds the position of, amongst others, Research Professor at the London School of Economics and Political Science and the School of Oriental and African Studies, Full Professor at Leiden University and Director of the Modern East Asia Research Centre, Full Professor at Groningen University and Director of the Centre for Development Studies. Ho is well-cited and published in leading journals of development, planning and area studies. He published numerous books, including with *Cambridge University Press, Oxford University Press,* and *Wiley Blackwell.* Ho achieved the William Kapp Prize, China Rural Development Award, and European Research Council Consolidator Grant. He chairs the International Conference on Agriculture and Rural Development (www.icardc .org) and sits on the boards of Land Use Policy, Conservation and Society, China Rural Economics, Journal of Peasant Studies, and other journals.

Servaas Storm
Delft University of Technology

Servaas Storm is a Dutch economist who has published widely on issues of macroeconomics, development, income distribution & economic growth, finance, and climate change. He is a Senior Lecturer at Delft University of Technology. He obtained a PhD in Economics (in 1992) from Erasmus University Rotterdam and worked as consultant for the ILO and UNCTAD. His latest book, co-authored with C.W.M. Naastepad, is *Macroeconomics Beyond the NAIRU* (Harvard University Press, 2012) and was awarded with the 2013 Myrdal Prize of the European Association for Evolutionary Political Economy. Servaas Storm is one of the editors of *Development and Change* (2006–now) and a member of the Institute for New Economic Thinking's Working Group on the Political Economy of Distribution.

Advisory Board

Arun Agrawal, *University of Michigan*
Jun Borras, *International Institute of Social Studies*
Daniel Bromley, *University of Wisconsin-Madison*
Jane Carruthers, *University of South Africa*
You-tien Hsing, *University of California, Berkeley*
Tamara Jacka, *Australian National University*

About the Series

The Cambridge Elements on Global Development Studies publishes ground-breaking, novel works that move beyond existing theories and methodologies of development in order to consider social change in real times and real spaces.

Cambridge Elements ≡

Global Development Studies

Elements in the Series

Printed in the United States
by Baker & Taylor Publisher Services